Chapter 1: Place Value 1

Grouping in fives: addition

We have met Mr Sweet who makes
choc-bars in his factory.
He packs 5 bars into a box.

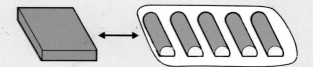

On the top shelf were
2 boxes and 2 bars
and on the bottom shelf
1 box and 4 bars.

But 6 bars are
1 box and 1 bar.

So he has:

Mr Sweet went to the store to see how many choc-bars he had.

boxes	bars
2	2
+ 1	4
3	6
4	1

If we use base 5 longs and units, we can do some more problems.

1 unit stands for 1 choc-bar.
1 long stands for 1 box.

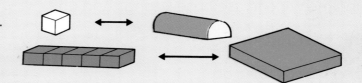

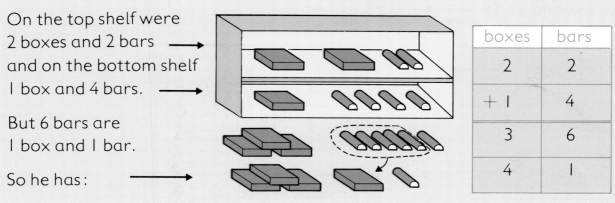

1 box 4 bars			▶		
1 box 2 bars					
2 boxes 6 bars			▶		
3 boxes 1 bar			▶		

1 Set out base 5 longs and units and work out these:

a boxes bars	**b** boxes bars	**c** boxes bars	**d** boxes bars
2 0	1 3	4	1 4
+ 1 3	+ 2 3	+ 1 2	+ 1 4

Grouping in sixes: addition

Mrs Giles packs eggs in boxes.
Each box holds 6 eggs.

On Sunday the hens
laid 8 eggs.
Mrs Giles put 6 into
a box so that she had
1 box and 2 eggs. ——→

On Monday the hens
laid 5 eggs. ——→

But she can put
6 eggs in
another box.
So she has: ——→

	boxes	eggs
	1	2
	+	5
	1	7
	2	1

This time we can use base 6 longs and units.

1 unit to stand for 1 egg.

1 long stands for 1 box.

Set out base 6 longs and units (or cubes which fit together to make
sticks of 6) and work out these:

1 a

boxes	eggs
1	3
+	5

c

boxes	eggs
2	4
+ 1	3

e

boxes	eggs
1	0
+	5

g

boxes	eggs
2	1
+ 2	5

b

boxes	eggs
2	5
+ 1	5

d

boxes	eggs
1	4
+ 3	4

f

boxes	eggs
1	2
+ 1	4

h

boxes	eggs
1	5
+	5

Using the multi-base board for addition

John is using squares, longs and units in the base four set.

A long is made from 4 units.

A square is made from 4 longs.

He sets out these on the multi-base board.

He records :

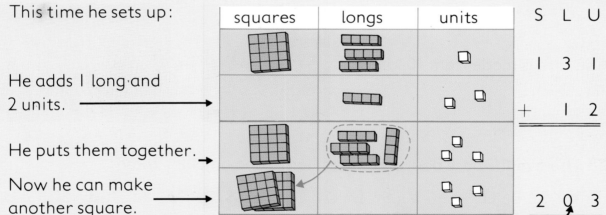

squares	longs	units

	S	L	U
	1	2	3
He adds 2 more units.	+		2
He puts them together.			
He makes another long. This is the answer :	1	3	1

He records :

squares	longs	units

	S	L	U
This time he sets up :	1	3	1
He adds 1 long and 2 units.	+	1	2
He puts them together.			
Now he can make another square.	2	0	3

The zero means there are no longs.

1 Use a multi-base board with squares, longs and units (base 4) to do these :

a
S	L	U
1	2	3
+		3

b
S	L	U
2	1	2
+	1	3

c
S	L	U
1	3	1
+1	1	1

d
S	L	U
1	0	3
+	1	1

In base five

A long is made from 5 units.

A square is made from 5 longs.

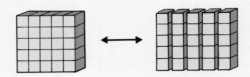

1 Use a multi-base board, squares, longs and units (base 5) for these:

	a S	L	U		**b** S	L	U		**c** S	L	U		**d** S	L	U
	1	1	2		1	2	2		2	2	3		2	1	4
+		1	4	+		4	1	+		1	3	+		4	2

In base ten

A long is made from 10 units.

A square is made from 10 longs.

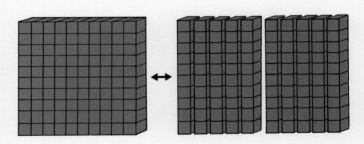

2 Use a multi-base board, squares, longs and units for these:

	a S	L	U		**b** S	L	U		**c** S	L	U		**d** S	L	U
	1	2	3			3	6			4	2			3	0
+		4	1	+		1	5	+		7	3	+		8	2

	e S	L	U		**f** S	L	U		**g** S	L	U		**h** S	L	U
	1	6	2			4	3	6			3	2		2	9	9
+		1	9	+	1	7	3	+		6	8	+	1	0	4

The abacus

An early abacus was made by placing pebbles in grooves. When the 'units' groove held ten pebbles, they were removed and one pebble was put in the 'tens' groove.

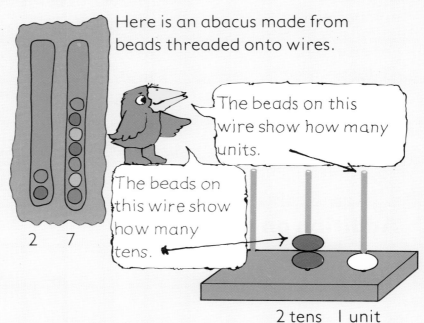

Here is an abacus made from beads threaded onto wires.

The beads on this wire show how many units.

The beads on this wire show how many tens.

This abacus shows 2 tens and 7 units or 27.

2 tens   1 unit

We can record any number on an abacus. (For large numbers we would need more wires.) Read these abacus numbers.

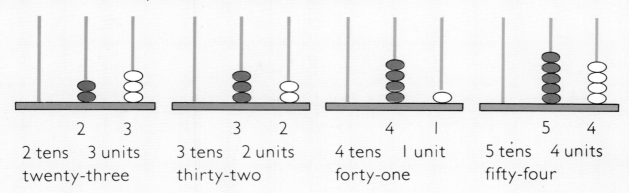

2   3
2 tens   3 units
twenty-three

3   2
3 tens   2 units
thirty-two

4   1
4 tens   1 unit
forty-one

5   4
5 tens   4 units
fifty-four

1 Copy these abacus pictures into your book and write the number they show.

a   b   c   d   e

2 Draw abacus pictures for these numbers:

a sixty-four   c eighty   e ninety-nine   g 7 tens and 3 units
b 50   d five   f five tens   h four tens and 2 units

A dash called a **hyphen** is used to join some number words.

For example,
43 forty-three
78 seventy-eight

1 Write these in words.

The words in the box will help you.

a 57   **e** 42
b 29   **f** 75
c 36   **g** 38
d 31   **h** 64

twenty	one
thirty	two
forty	three
fifty	four
sixty	five
seventy	six
eighty	seven
ninety	eight
	nine

Addition on the abacus

For example: 13 + 2 = 15

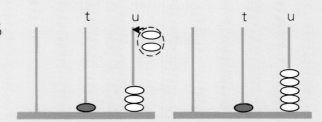

27 + 5

This column is full so we exchange ten beads for one and put it on the tens.

Now put on the other two units to make:

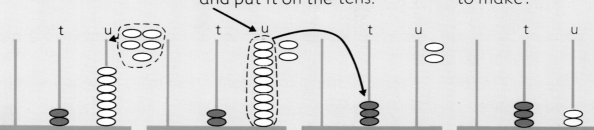

2 Use your abacus to do these additions.
Draw an abacus picture of each answer.

a 17 + 2   **e** 49 + 1   **i** 38 + 2 tens   **m** sixteen + twelve
b 22 + 6   **f** 35 + 10   **j** 52 + 17   **n** 69 + 1
c 24 + 10   **g** forty-four + 7   **k** seven + twelve   **o** 40 + 40
d 19 + 2   **h** 45 + 1 ten   **l** seventy + twelve   **p** eighteen + 13

3 Add 10 to each of these numbers: 5, 9, 20, 12, 23, 90.

Chapter 2: Addition 1

Adding tens

The abacus shows 3 tens. 2 more tens are put on 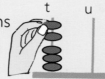 to make 5 tens or fifty.

$$\begin{array}{r} 30 \\ +20 \\ \hline 50 \end{array}$$

The counting board shows:

tens	units
4 tens	
and 3 tens	

→ 40
→ 30
—
70
—

→

tens	units

and 3 tens added together to give 7 tens.

I Copy and complete. Use an abacus or counting board.

a 50+20 =   **c** 7 tens+20 =   **e** 10+40+20+10 =

b 30+60 =   **d** 30+2 tens =   **f** 2 tens+40+3 tens =

Adding tens and units

Follow the pictures to see how the counting board is used to add 32 and 25.

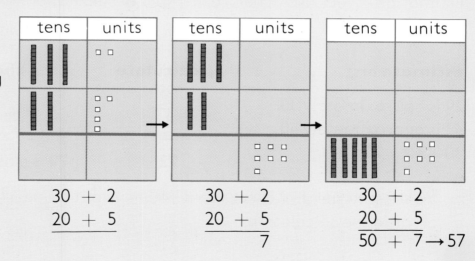

$$\begin{array}{r} 30 + 2 \\ 20 + 5 \\ \hline \end{array}$$

$$\begin{array}{r} 30 + 2 \\ 20 + 5 \\ \hline 7 \end{array}$$

$$\begin{array}{r} 30 + 2 \\ 20 + 5 \\ \hline 50 + 7 \rightarrow 57 \end{array}$$

2 Do these the same way:

a $\begin{array}{r} 43 \\ +22 \\ \hline \end{array}$ **b** $\begin{array}{r} 57 \\ +12 \\ \hline \end{array}$ **c** $\begin{array}{r} 61 \\ +25 \\ \hline \end{array}$ **d** $\begin{array}{r} 20 \\ +69 \\ \hline \end{array}$ **e** $\begin{array}{r} 54 \\ +42 \\ \hline \end{array}$ **f** $\begin{array}{r} 47 \\ +41 \\ \hline \end{array}$ **g** $\begin{array}{r} 63 \\ +36 \\ \hline \end{array}$

Estimation to the nearest 10

An estimate is very useful. It tells you roughly what sort of result to expect. An estimate is not the exact number but it is close.

We estimate to the nearest 'round' or **approximate** number using the **Halfway Rule**.

Rounding to the nearest 10 (that is 10,20,30,40, ...)

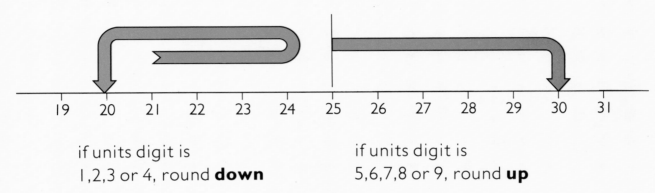

if units digit is
1,2,3 or 4, round **down**

if units digit is
5,6,7,8 or 9, round **up**

For example, 24 rounds **down** to 20 and 37 rounds **up** to 40.

1   Round these numbers up or down to the nearest 10:

a 46   **b** 19   **c** 33   **d** 87   **e** 12   **f** 43   **g** 51   **h** 28   **i** 45

Estimation is very useful before any sort of calculation.
For example: 29 + 43

estimate first	then **calculate**	then **check**
29 is approximately 30	29	
43 is approximately 40	+ 43	
30 + 40 = **70**	———	
	72	**70** is close to **72**

Your estimate of 70 checks that you have not made a large error in the calculation

2   Write **two results** for each of these — an estimate, by rounding to the nearest 10, and the exact answer. Check by comparing them.

a 33	**b** 18	**c** 62	**d** 25	**e** 58	**f** 42	**g** 61
+ 26	+ 31	+ 25	+ 62	+ 41	+ 47	+ 36
——	——	——	——	——	——	——

Remember to estimate first by rounding numbers to the nearest 10.
Use the counting
board for 27 + 15.

Set out 27 as 20 + 7 ⟶

and 15 as 10 + 5 ⟶

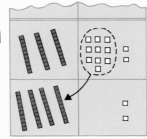

tens	units

Add them together:

3 tens and 12 units   30 + 12
Exchange 10 units for 1 ten-rod
and put it in the tens column.
30 + 10 + 2

4 tens and 2 units ⟶ 42

1 Do these in the
same way.

a	54	**e**	75
	+27		+18

b	56	**f**	69
	+38		+21

c	63	**g**	46
	+29		+37

d	45	**h**	83
	+37		+ 9

2 Try these **without** using rods or the abacus. Copy and complete:

a 36 ➔ ☐ + 6
+25 ➔ 20 + ☐
50 + 11 ➔ 50 + ☐ + ☐ ➔ 61

b 47 ➔ ☐ + ☐
+26 ➔ ☐ + ☐
60 + ☐ ➔ 60 + ☐ + 3 ➔ ☐

Use the same method for these:

c	44	**d**	66	**e**	46	**f**	33	**g**	65	**h**	52
	+18		+28		+46		+27		+26		+38

Here is another
way to set out
your work.

```
  28
+47
  15 (8+7)
  60 (20+40)
  75
```

3 Copy and complete:

a
```
  46
+38
  14 (☐+8)
  70 (40+☐)
  84
```

b
```
  65
+26
  ☐ (5+6)
  ☐ (60+20)
  ☐
```

c	74	**d**	57	**e**	48	**f**	51	**g**	66	**h**	58
	+18		+36		+19		+39		+28		+27

Remember to estimate first by rounding numbers to the nearest 10.

An even shorter way of recording what happens on the counting board is:

8+7 = 15; put the 5 units in the answer.
Record the 'ten' below the line in the tens column.
Add the tens; 20+10 = 30 and 1 ten below the line makes 4 tens.

```
 28
+17
 45
  1
```

> Don't forget the ten under the tens column.

1 Use the shorter method for these:

a 67		**c** 39		**e** 48		**g** 56		**i** 75		**k** 23
+25		+29		+37		+ 9		+15		+55

b 76		**d** 16		**f** 38		**h** 44		**j** 64		**l** 38
+17		+24		+29		+25		+29		+32

Sometimes there may be more than two numbers to add together.
Use the same way as before but be extra careful.
Always estimate first and check your answer.

```
 42
+26
 17
 85
  1
```

2 Now try these:

a 44	**b** 56	**c** 48	**d** 46	**e** 69	**f** 28
+33	+25	+20	.+28	+ 9	+26
16	18	24	17	20	25
					17

Sometimes you may have to put the figures in columns yourself. For example: Add these numbers.

In addition, the answer is called the **sum** or **total**.

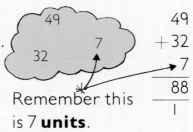

Remember this is 7 **units**.

```
 49
+32
  7
 88
  1
```

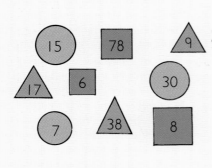

3 Find the total of the numbers:

a in the squares,
b in the triangles,
c in the circles.
d What is the grand total of all the numbers?

Remember to estimate first by rounding numbers to the nearest 10.

Try these addition problems.
The first one is set out for you.

$$\begin{array}{r} 13 \\ +33 \\ 3 \\ \hline \\ \hline \end{array}$$

Set the problems out like this.

1 **a** Add thirteen, thirty-three and three.

  b Find the sum of fourteen, four and forty-four.

  c Add twenty-five, thirty-five and fifteen.

  d What is the total when twenty-one, seventeen and nineteen are added?

  e Eighteen plus twenty-seven plus thirty-one gives what total?

  f Mary spent 37 pence at the grocer's, 25 pence at the sweet shop and 28 pence at the baker's. How much did she spend altogether?

  g Peter has collected 49 British stamps, 24 French stamps and 8 German. What is his total number of stamps?

  h Mrs Giles collected 17 eggs on Monday, 8 on Tuesday, 11 on Wednesday and 19 on Thursday. How many eggs did she collect altogether?

Magic squares

16	9	14
11	13	15
12	17	10

2 Add the numbers in each row.
Add the numbers in each column.
Add the numbers in each diagonal.

3 Add 7 to the number in each cell to make a new magic square. Draw it in your book.
What is the new total for each row, column and diagonal?
Try adding other numbers to each cell.

4 Check that this is a magic square.

16	2	3	13
5	11	10	8
9	7	6	12
4	14	15	1

5 Work out and write in your book the numbers missing in this magic square.

14	9	13	
	11	7	16
3	12	8	15
17	6	10	5

Chapter 3: Shape 1

Turning

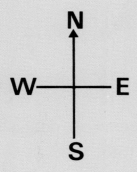

If I stand facing North and turn through one complete turn, I shall be facing North again.

If I start by facing North and turn through half a complete turn, I shall be facing South.

If I start by facing North and turn to my right through a quarter of a turn, I shall be facing East.

If I start by facing North and turn to my left through a quarter of a complete turn, I shall be facing West.

I Copy and complete.

I start facing:	I turn through:	direction	I finish facing:
South	A complete turn		
East	$\frac{1}{2}$ a complete turn		
West	$\frac{1}{4}$ of a complete turn	right	
South	$\frac{1}{4}$ of a complete turn	left	
West	A complete turn		
South	$\frac{1}{2}$ of a complete turn		
East	$\frac{1}{4}$ of a complete turn	right	
West	$\frac{1}{4}$ of a complete turn	left	
East	A complete turn		
West	$\frac{1}{2}$ of a complete turn		
South	$\frac{3}{4}$ of a complete turn	right	
East	$\frac{3}{4}$ of a complete turn	left	

Fold a circle of paper or thin card into four. Open it out and mark in the points.

As a pointer push a pipecleaner or straw up through the centre. (Bend it over at the back.)

Use the pointer to check your answers to question 1.

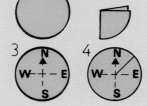

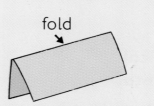

One quarter of a complete
turn has a special name – a **right angle**.
It is called a right angle because it is
a true angle which makes a square corner.

1 Take a piece of paper, any shape,
and fold it roughly in half.
Now fold it in half again.

fold

The corner where the folds meet
is a **right angle**.

right angle

2 Use your right angle to find things in your classroom which have right
angles for their corners. Make a list.

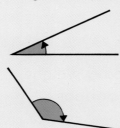

A turn which is less than a right angle is called
an **acute angle**.

A turn which is more than one right angle but less
than two right angles is called an **obtuse angle**.

3 Use your folded right angle to complete the sentences. The first
is done for you.

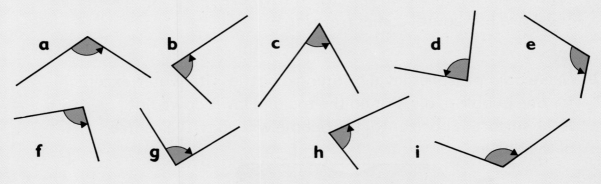

Angle **a** is [obtuse.] Angle **d** is [   ] Angle **g** is [   ]
Angle **b** is [   ] Angle **e** is [   ] Angle **h** is [   ]
Angle **c** is [   ] Angle **f** is [   ] Angle **i** is [   ]

Vertical and horizontal

Crooked houses are fun to visit
but not such fun to live in.

Can you see what is wrong with
this house?

Builders must make sure that the walls
are upright or **vertical**
and level or **horizontal**.

To make sure the walls are **vertical**
the builder uses a **plumb line**.

To make sure that they are
horizontal he uses a **spirit level**.

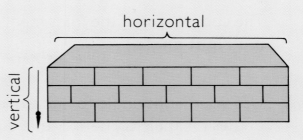

1   Make a plumb line from a piece of string with a small heavy weight
    at the end. Hold your plumb line by the side of the wall or door.
    Are the wall and the frame of the door vertical?
    Find some other verticals in the classroom.

    No matter how you tilt a container with
    water in it, the surface of the water remains
    level or horizontal. Can you discover where
    the word horizontal comes from?

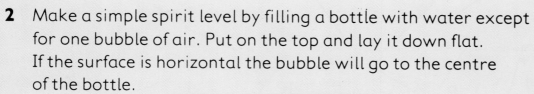

2   Make a simple spirit level by filling a bottle with water except
    for one bubble of air. Put on the top and lay it down flat.
    If the surface is horizontal the bubble will go to the centre
    of the bottle.

    Use your spirit level to test some of the surfaces in
    your classroom to see if they are horizontal.

1 Partly fill a jar with water and
hold your plumb line in front of
the jar.
Look at the water level.

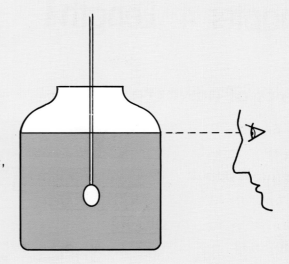

Can you say what angles you see,
where your vertical line crosses
your horizontal line?
Use your folded right angle to
measure them.

Vertical and horizontal lines meet or cross at right angles.
We say that they are **perpendicular** to one another.

2 John was asked by his teacher
to run and touch the wall
as quickly as he could.

Which path did he take?
Why?

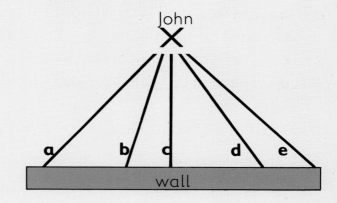

Copy this sentence putting in the missing word.

John's path and the wall are [   ] to each other.

3 Copy and complete the sentence.

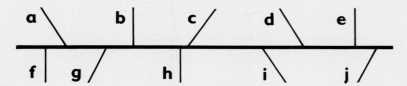

In the diagram, the lines perpendicular to the thick line are [   ]

4 Draw a line 8 cm long and draw four lines
which are perpendicular to it.

Chapter 4: Length 1

Parts of a metre

You need:
a metre stick,
2 strips of paper
50cm long,
and 1 strip
10cm long.

Remember:
cm means centimetre
or centimetres.
m means metre or metres.

1 Copy and complete.
   a There are ☐ 50cm strips in 1 metre.
   b Each 50 cm strip is ☐ a metre.
   c There are ☐ 10cm strips in 1 metre.
   d There are ☐ 10cm strips in $\frac{1}{2}$ metre.

Now cut one of your 50cm strips in half.

2 Copy and complete.
   a Each half of the 50cm strip is about ☐ cm long.
   b There are ☐ 25cm strips in 1 metre.
   c Each one is a qu ‾ ‾ ‾ ‾ ‾ of a metre.

3 Copy and complete. The first one is done for you.
   a 5 lots of 10cm = $\frac{1}{2}$ m or 50 cm
   b $\frac{1}{2}$m — 25cm = △m or ☐ cm
   c 50cm — $\frac{1}{4}$ m = △m or ☐ cm
   d $\frac{1}{2}$m + $\frac{1}{4}$m + $\frac{1}{4}$m = △m or ☐ cm

   e 1m — $\frac{1}{4}$m = △m or ☐ cm
   f $\frac{1}{4}$m + $\frac{1}{4}$m + 10cm = ☐ cm
   g $\frac{1}{2}$m — 10cm = ☐ cm
   h 1m — 10cm = ☐ cm

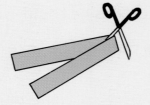

4 Use your 50cm, 25cm and 10cm strips to measure objects in your classroom. Make a list of at least 3 objects in each column.

Record like this:

Less than 10cm	10cm to 25cm	25cm to 50cm	50cm to 1m
rubber	book	desk	blackboard

The snail race

Three snails, Ali, Bess and Con, started
at the same time to crawl along a path.
The picture shows how far they had
gone after 1 hour.

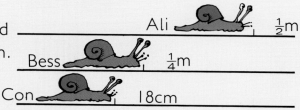

Ali $\frac{1}{2}$m

Bess $\frac{1}{4}$m

Con 18cm

1 Copy and complete:
In one hour:
    a Ali crawled ☐ cm farther than Bess.
    b Bess went ☐ cm farther than Con.
    c Ali went ☐ cm farther than Con.
    d ☐ crawled the farthest.
    e ☐ crawled the shortest distance.
    f The fastest snail was ☐
    g The slowest snail was ☐

The perimeter

Put your finger on the start
and follow the arrows.
The distance all around the shape
is called the perimeter.
The perimeter of this shape is 14cm.

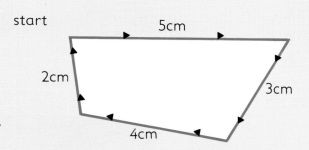

start

5cm

2cm

3cm

4cm

2 Work out the perimeters of these shapes:

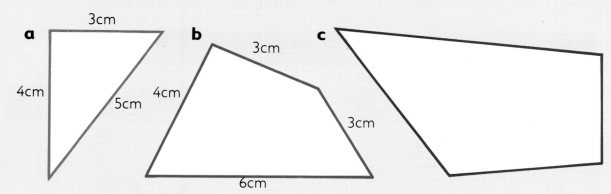

a 3cm, 4cm, 5cm

b 3cm, 4cm, 6cm

c 3cm

3 Use your ruler to find the perimeter of some objects in your classroom.
Record like this:

object	lengths of the sides	perimeter
book	15cm + 20cm + 15cm + 20cm	70cm

The decimetre (10cm) strip

Carefully measure
and cut out a strip
of card 10cm long.

10 cm

Check that the strip fits 10 times along the metre rule.
This means the strip is one tenth of a metre long.
It is a decimetre strip ("deci" means "tenth").

$$10 \, cm = 1 \text{ decimetre (dm)} = \tfrac{1}{10} \text{ metre}$$

1   Copy and complete:
   a   1 decimetre = ☐ cm
   b   2 decimetres = ☐ cm
   c   4 decimetres = ☐ cm
   d   5 decimetres = ☐ cm
   e   6dm   = ☐ cm
   f   7dm   = ☐ cm
   g   9dm   = ☐ cm
   h   10dm   = ☐ cm

Carefully mark off your decimetre strip into centimetres.

1	2	3	4	5	6	7	8	9	10

2   The length of this pencil is 1dm strip and 4cm 'left over'.

Use your decimetre strip to measure objects in the classroom.
Record like this:

object	number of dm strips	cm "left over"	total measurement
pencil	1	4	14cm
width of this book	2	1	21cm

Chapter 5: Addition 2

Introducing the hundred

I is added to
99 to make 100.

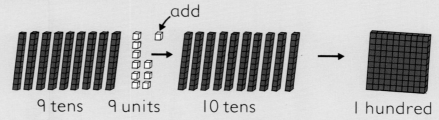

add

9 tens   9 units   10 tens   1 hundred

On an abacus, 99 is recorded like this:

If 1 unit is added, there are ten units. add 1 ◯

The 10 units are exchanged for 1 ten to make 10

The 10 tens are exchanged for 1 hundred.

Two hundred and thirty-six can be written as 236. It looks like this in squares, longs and units.

hundreds	tens	units

It can be recorded like this on an abacus.

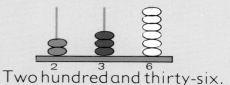

2   3   6

Two hundred and thirty-six.

1 Here are some numbers set out in squares, longs and units.
Draw an abacus picture.
Write the numbers in figures and words.

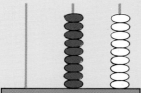

a

hundreds	tens	units

b

hundreds	tens	units

c

hundreds	tens	units

d

hundreds	tens	units

e

hundreds	tens	units

1 Copy these abacus pictures and write the number they show in words and figures.

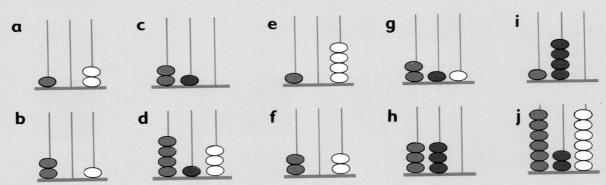

2 Draw abacus pictures for these and write the numbers in figures underneath.
  a Two hundred and nineteen   **e** Three hundred and seventy
  b One hundred and five   **f** Seven hundred and one
  c Eighty-seven   **g** One hundred and thirty
  d Two hundred and twenty-four **h** Two hundred and twelve

3 Add 1 to each of these numbers.
Draw an abacus picture of your answer, and write it in words and figures.
For example: 211 + 1

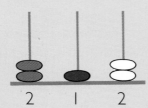

2   1   2

two hundred and twelve

a 100	**e** 234	**i** 109
b 103	**f** 310	**j** 209
c 120	**g** 99	**k** 229
d 219	**h** 409	**l** 499

4 Add 10 to each of these numbers.
Draw an abacus picture of your answer, and write it in words and figures.
For example: 105 + 10

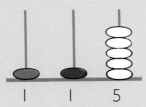

1   1   5

One hundred and fifteen

a 201	**e** 890	**i** 301
b 7	**f** 299	**j** 96
c 111	**g** 219	**k** 509
d 57	**h** 394	**l** 90

Adding hundreds, tens and units

Follow the picture diagrams to see how the counting board can be used to add 254 and 169.

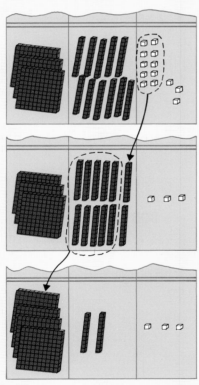

Set out 254 $200 + 50 + 4$

and 169 $100 + 60 + 9$

Add them together.

$300 + 110 + 13$

Exchange 10 units for 1 ten rod.

$300 + 110 + 10 + 3$

Exchange 10 ten rods for 1 hundred square.

$300 + 100 + 10 + 10 + 3$

423 $400 + 20 + 3$

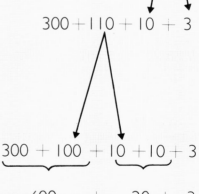

I   Use some squares, longs and units on a counting board to do these.

	a	**b**	**c**	**d**	**e**
	256	374	287	463	256
	+128	+163	+184	+177	+447

Estimation to the nearest 100

For hundreds, tens and units we estimate to the nearest
hundred (100, 200, 300, 400, ...) using the **Halfway Rule**.
This time, 50 is the halfway mark.

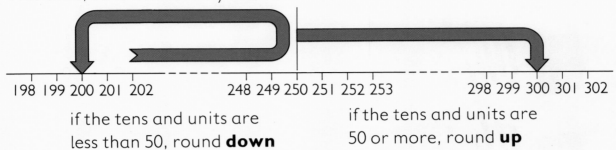

198 199 200 201 202   248 249 250 251 252 253   298 299 300 301 302

if the tens and units are
less than 50, round **down**

if the tens and units are
50 or more, round **up**

For example 234 rounds **down** to 200 and 568 rounds **up** to 600

1 Round these numbers up or down to the nearest 100:
    a 170   **b** 384   **c** 225   **d** 471   **e** 750   **f** 919   **g** 150   **h** 76

Remember it is always a good idea to estimate before calculating.
For example: $526 + 263$

estimate first	then **calculate**	then **check**
526 is approximately 500	526	
263 is approximately 300	+ 263	
$500 + 300 = \mathbf{800}$	———	
	789	**800** is close to **789**

2 Write **two results** for each of these — an estimate, by rounding to the
nearest 100, and an exact answer. Check by comparing them.
    a   179   **b**   350   **c**   601   **d**   149   **e**   452
      + 220   + 238   + 215   + 150   + 30

The round number we estimate to depends on the size of the number:
flowers in a bunch, nearest 10; pages in a book, nearest 100;
people at a Cup Final, nearest 1000 (the halfway mark is 500.)

3 How would you estimate these — to the nearest 10, 100 or 1000?
    a books on a shelf   **d** children in a class
    b lines on a page   **e** children in a school
    c words in a dictionary   **f** bricks in a wall

Remember to estimate first by rounding numbers to the nearest 100.

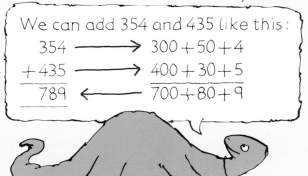

We can add 354 and 435 like this:

$$354 \longrightarrow 300+50+4$$
$$+435 \longrightarrow 400+30+5$$
$$\overline{789} \longleftarrow \overline{700+80+9}$$

1 Set these out in the same way.

a	253	**c**	172	**e**	348
	+145		+206		+151

b	505	**d**	316	**f**	147
	+272		+ 82		+741

Now look at this:

$$258 \longrightarrow 200 + 50 + 8$$
$$+179 \longrightarrow 100 + 70 + 9$$
$$\overline{ 300 + 120 + 17}$$

$$300 + 100 + 20 + 10 + 7$$

$$437 \longleftarrow 400 + 30 + 7$$

2 Set these out in the same way.

a	575	**c**	493	**e**	708
	+319		+472		+199

b	428	**d**	254	**f**	675
	+315		+ 89		+146

Here is another way to set out your work:

$$
\begin{array}{r}
378 \\
+149 \\
\hline
17 \quad (8+9) \\
110 \quad (70+40) \\
400 \quad (300+100) \\
\hline
527
\end{array}
$$

3 Set these out like the example.

a	675	**c**	765	**e**	829
	+279		+295		+198

b	706	**d**	438	**f**	497
	+284		+362		+303

There is an even shorter way of recording addition.

$$
\begin{array}{r}
378 \\
+149 \\
\hline
527 \\
11
\end{array}
$$

8+9 =17. Put the 7 units in the answer.

Record the "ten" below the line in the tens column.

7 tens + 4 tens + 1 ten = 12 tens.

Put the 2 tens in the answer.

Record the "hundred" below the line in the hundreds column.

Add the hundreds.

4 Do these, using the shorter way of recording.

a	485	**b**	392	**c**	640	**d**	723	**e**	635	**f**	186
	+276		+288		+272		+190		+ 84		+235

Remember — estimate, calculate, check.

1 Try these addition problems.

a Add four hundred and four,
forty-four,
fourteen.

$$\begin{array}{r} 404 \\ 44 \\ +\ 14 \\ \hline \end{array}$$

Be sure to put the figures in the correct columns. The first one is set out for you.

b Add five hundred and fifty, fifteen, fifty-five.
c Find the total of forty-six, fifty-six, sixty-six.
d Add one hundred and eight, eighty, eighteen.

Write the answers to these.

2 a I more than 199   **b** 20 less than 112   **c** 2 more than 85
    d Find the total of your answers to **a**, **b**, and **c**.

3 a 2 less than 201   **b** 20 less than 102   **c** 200 less than 320
    d Find the total of your answers to **a**, **b** and **c**.

4 a At Woodlands Infant School there are 84 girls and 103 boys.
How many children are there at the Infant School?
   b At Woodlands Junior School there are 159 girls and 142 boys.
How many children are there in the Junior School?
   c How many boys are there altogether in the Infant and Junior School?
   d How many girls are there altogether in the Infant and Junior School?
   e What is the total number of children in both schools?

5 First estimate, then find out about the number of children in your
school and answer questions like those in **4**.

6 Work out the missing numbers in these magic squares:

a

136	17	
	85	119
68	153	

b

181	27	38	148
	126	115	
104		71	137
49	159	170	16

Chapter 6: Co-ordinates

Routes

This diagram shows a route marked from **A** to **B** moving along the lines. The side of a square is 1 unit.

1 **a** How long is this route?
   b Is this the **shortest** route along the lines?
   c Is there more than one shortest route?

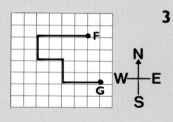

2 **a** How long is this route?
   b On a small piece of squared paper draw a route 7 units long.
   c Draw a route 9 units long.

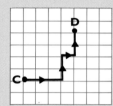

3 This diagram shows one way of getting from **G** to **F** travelling along the lines.
   a How long is it?
   b How long is the shortest route?
   Using the points of the compass we can write this route as 3 West, 2 North, 2 West, 2 North, 4 East or 3W, 2N, 2W, 2N, 4E.

c Find three other ways of getting from **G** to **F**.
   Write down in your book the directions your routes took.
d Write down a route from **F** to **G** in which all the letters N,E,W,S are used.

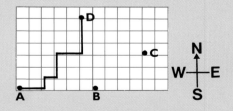

4 The route from **A** to **D** can be written as: 2E, 1N, 1E, 2N, 2E, 3N.

a Copy this route onto squared paper.
b Start at **B** and draw this route on your squared paper: 2N, 1E, 4N, 2W
c Make up a code for yourself showing any route you could use to get from **C** to **B**. (It does not matter if it touches another route.)

Finding a point

Street guides only say what square a street is in.
If we number lines instead of spaces, then our addresses
will be points where the lines cross.

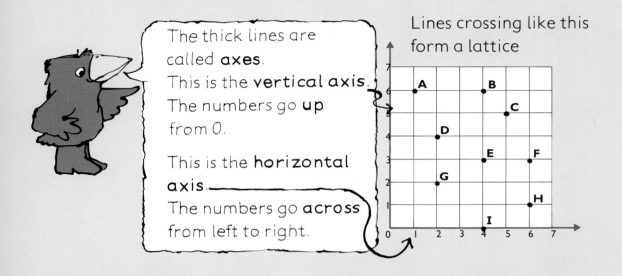

The thick lines are called **axes**.
This is the **vertical axis**.
The numbers go **up** from 0.

This is the **horizontal axis**.
The numbers go **across** from left to right.

Lines crossing like this form a lattice

I These addresses at exact points are called **co-ordinates**.
Start at 0, the **origin**. Count the lines across and then up.
Here the co-ordinates of **A** are (1,6) or 1 across, 6 up,
B is at (4,6), **C** is at (5,5).
Write in your book the co-ordinates of **D**, **E**, **F**, **G**, **H** and **I**.

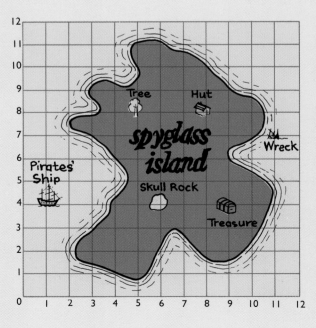

Here is a map of Spyglass Island.
The pirates used it to find
the buried treasure.

2 Write in your book the
co-ordinates of:

a the pirates' ship
b Skull Rock
c the tree
d the hut
e the wreck
f the treasure.

Here is another map.
Look at it and see if you can answer these questions about it.

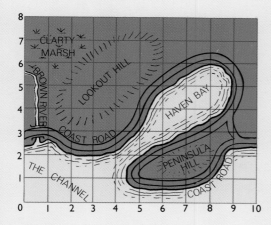

I **a** Would a good place for a
lighthouse be at (7,2)?

  b If my car was at (5,3), would
I be annoyed?

  c To go from (3,2) to (5,1) would it
be shorter to go by car or boat?

  d Could someone at (2,7) see
someone at (7,3)?

2 Make up your own map, and write a story to go with it.

Joining points

Make a lattice like this on squared paper. Number the lines, not the spaces.
Number the horizontal axis (left to right) from
0 to 12 and the vertical axis (bottom to top) from 0 to 8.

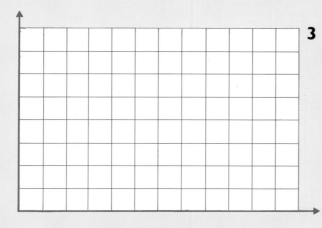

3 Mark these points on your
lattice and join each to the point
which follows it. Inside each
shape, write its name.

  a (7,6) (12,6) (8,8) (7,6)
  b (10,0) (12,3) (9,5) (7,2) (10,0)
  c (4,7) (6,1) (1,5) (7,5) (2,1) (4,7)

4 Make another lattice on squared paper like the last one.
Mark and join these points in order:
(4,7) (2,7) (1,6) (0,4) (2,3) (3,4) (4,3) (4,0) (5,0) (5,2) (6,3) (9,3) (10,2)
(10,0) (11,0) (11,2) (12,4) (12,5) (9,8) (8,7) (9,7) (10,6) (5,6) (4,7) (3,5) (2,7)
Make up another picture and give to your friends the list of co-ordinates
from which to draw the picture.

Chapter 7: Money 1

The pound

The £1 coin was introduced
on 21st April 1983.
It replaced the old
£1 note which wore out
too quickly.

1   Find out why the word pound and the symbol £ are used for
    money. Why is it sometimes called the pound Sterling?

2   Look at a £1 coin.
    Whose picture do you see on the front of it?
    What design is on the back?
    Are all £1 coins exactly the same?

3   What is written round the edge of £1 coins?
    Are the words always the same?
    Find out what the words mean.

How £1 is made up

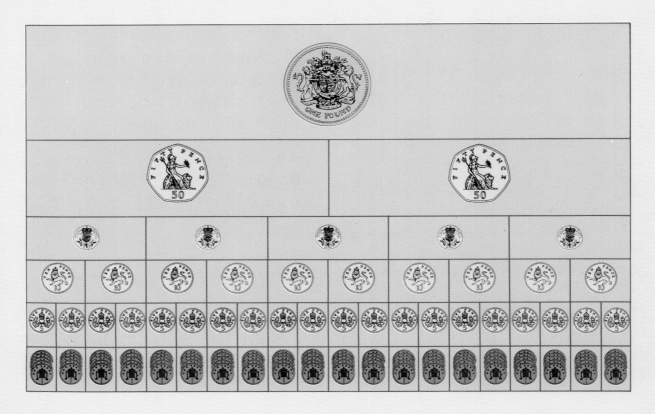

1 Copy and complete these sentences.

a ☐ 50p coins have the same value as £1.
b ☐ 10p coins have the same value as £1.
c ☐ 5p coins have the same value as £1.
d ☐ 10p coins have the same value as a 50p coin.
e ☐ 5p coins have the same value as a 50p coin.
f 10 1p coins have the same value as ☐ 5p coins.
g 30 1p coins have the same value as ☐ 10p coins.

Reading amounts more than £1

To buy things, you often need a mixture of pounds and pence. When recording, the pounds and pence are kept separate.

Here we have one pound and 34 pence.

This is recorded as £1·34.

The decimal point separates the pounds from the pence and we do not write p after the pence.

Here is another example:

Three pounds and 67 pence is written as £3·67.

2 Record the following in the same way.

a One pound and 23 pence.
b Three pounds and 18 pence.
c Two pounds and 52 pence.
d Five pounds and 81 pence.
e Three pounds and 80 pence.
f Seven pounds and 14 pence.
g Four pounds and 58 pence.
h Ten pounds and 79 pence.

Recording money on an abacus

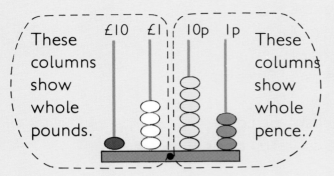

The abacus shows
one £10 and four £1s,
six 10 pences and three pence.
That makes fourteen pounds
and sixty-three pence.

We record it as £14·63

1   Write down the amounts shown on each abacus.

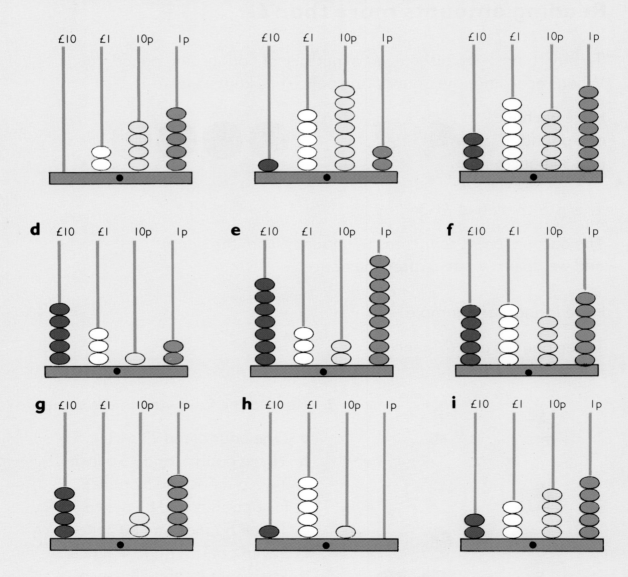

2   Draw an abacus to record each of the following prices.
    a £2·34   **b** £4·23   **c** £16·81   **d** £6·38   **e** £14·64

Giving change up to £1

If you spend 38p in a shop and give the shopkeeper £1 in payment,
he must give you some change.
He usually does it this way.

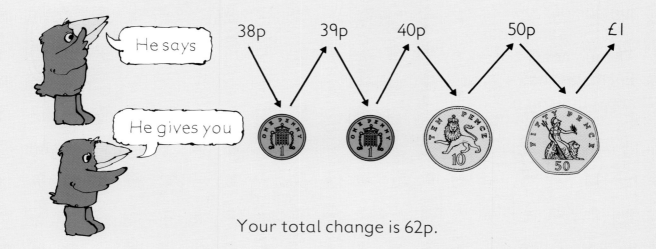

Your total change is 62p.

1   What change do you get from £1 if you spend
the following amounts?
Use your coins. The first one is done for you.

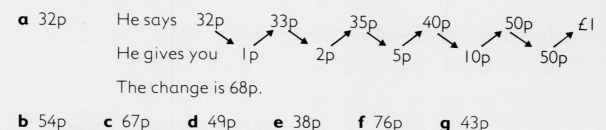

a 32p

He says   32p   33p   35p   40p   50p   £1

He gives you   1p   2p   5p   10p   50p

The change is 68p.

b 54p   **c** 67p   **d** 49p   **e** 38p   **f** 76p   **g** 43p

2   Copy and complete the following additions.
Estimate first by rounding to the nearest £ (midway mark 50p).

a £1·23 +£2·34	**d** £2·79 +£3·50	**g** £3·72 +£2·19	**j** £16·73 +£19·48
b £3·81 +£2·45	**e** £4·53 +£2·45	**h** £6·23 +£3·49	**k** £13·91 +£ 8·49
c £1·53 +£3·42	**f** £4·32 +£1·89	**i** £13·27 +£ 9·46	**l** £17·44 +£34·78

Chapter 8: Volume and Capacity 1

How much is 100ml?

Here is a big measuring jug, full of fruit drink, and some small glasses. The jug holds 1 litre. Each glass holds 100 millilitres (100ml).

When a glass is filled from the jug, the level in the jug goes down like this:

1 How many glasses can be filled from the jug?
Draw a jug like this one and mark 100ml sections down the side.

Using the 100ml measure

Take a 100ml measure and five milk bottles.
Use the measure and a funnel to put water in the bottles:

100ml in bottle 1
200ml in bottle 2
300ml in bottle 3
400ml in bottle 4
500ml in bottle 5

(If you tap them with a pencil you can play a tune.)

2 In your book, write down the total amounts in:
  a bottles 1 and 3
  b bottles 3 and 5
  c bottles 1, 3 and 4
  d bottles 2, 3 and 5

3 a How much more is in bottle 5 than in bottle 3?
  b How much more is in bottle 4 than in bottle 2?
  c How much must you pour from bottle 3 into bottle 1, so that there will be the same amount in bottles 1, 2 and 3?

Very small measures

A hollow cube with sides 1 centimetre long
holds 1 millilitre.

That is why this very small amount is sometimes
called 1 cubic centimetre.

This should be written as 1 cm³.

Capacities are sometimes measured in cubic centimetres,
for example the size of motor bike or car engines.

The amount of space something takes up is called its **volume**.
The volume of this cube is 1 cm³.

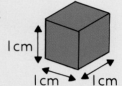

1   Use centimetre cubes to build these solids.
    Find their volumes in cm³ by counting the cubes:

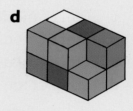

a   **b** 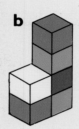   **c** 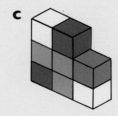   **d**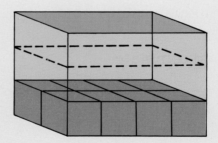

There are 8 cm³ in the bottom layer.
There is room for 3 layers.
$8 \times 3 = 24$
so the box holds 24 cm³.

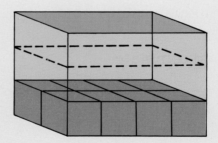

2   Use centimetre cubes to find how many cm³ these boxes will hold.

a 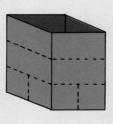   **b** 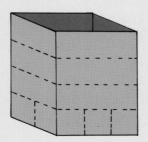   **c**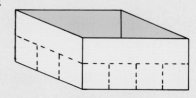

1 A medicine spoon holds 5ml.

Estimate first then use a medicine spoon to measure the capacity of small containers in millilitres.

Record like this:

container	estimate	measure
egg cup wine glass yoghurt pot	ml	ml

2 How many ml of medicine would you swallow, if you took:

a 1 spoonful a day for 5 days?   **c** 2 spoonfuls a day for a week?
b 2 spoonfuls a day for 5 days?   **d** 3 spoonfuls a day for 10 days?

3 Copy and complete

a 20ml of medicine is ☐ 5ml spoonfuls.
b 15ml of medicine is ☐ 5ml spoonfuls.
c 50ml of medicine is ☐ 5ml spoonfuls.
d 100ml of medicine is ☐ 5ml spoonfuls.

Look at the labels of some medicine bottles and find out how many spoonfuls they hold.

4 Copy and complete

size of bottle	50ml	100ml	150ml	200ml	300ml	500ml
number of 5ml spoonfuls						

The hollow centimetre cube (1ml) and the medicine spoon (5ml) are too small for measuring the capacity of most containers.

You would have to use the hollow cm cube about 270 times or the spoon about 54 times to fill a beaker!

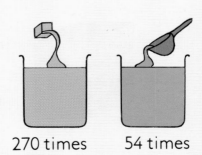

270 times   54 times

Making a 100ml measure

A handy size for a measure is
100 millilitres (100ml) or 100 cubic centimetres (100cm³).

Use 1cm cubes or Cuisenaire rods
to see what 100cm³ looks like.

First make a square layer 5cm by 5cm.

Four layers like this make 100cm³ or 100ml.

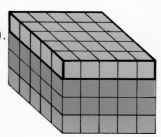

4 layers: $25 \times 4 = 100$cm³

To make 100ml measure, cut the top from
an empty plastic container (washing-up liquid bottle).

Pour 100ml of water from a measuring jug into the
container.

Carefully mark the water level, empty the water out
and cut round the container on the mark.

water level mark

plastic container
cut to hold 100ml.

You can make a 100ml measure from
card or centimetre squared paper:

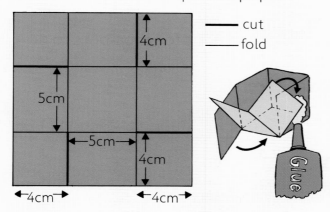

—— cut
—— fold

5cm   5cm   4cm
4cm   4cm

I When you have made your
measure, use it with some
sand to find the capacity of:

a a jam jar   **b** a beaker
c a small box

Record the results in
your book.

1 litre (1000ml) of water weighs 1kg (1000 grams).

1ml of water weighs 1 gram.

100ml of water weighs 1 hecto (100 grams).

If your 100ml container holds water,
weigh it and see.
(It may not quite balance because of the weight
of the container.)

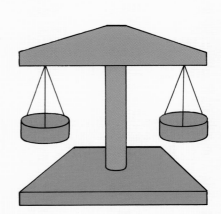

Chapter 9: Place Value 2

Grouping in fives: subtraction

One day Mr Sweet wanted 4 choc-bars for prizes at a party.
In the store he had 2 boxes of 5 choc-bars and I single choc-bar.

I want to take away 4 bars, so I must open up a box.
Now I have I box and 6 bars.

I can take away 4 bars.
That leaves I box and 2 bars.

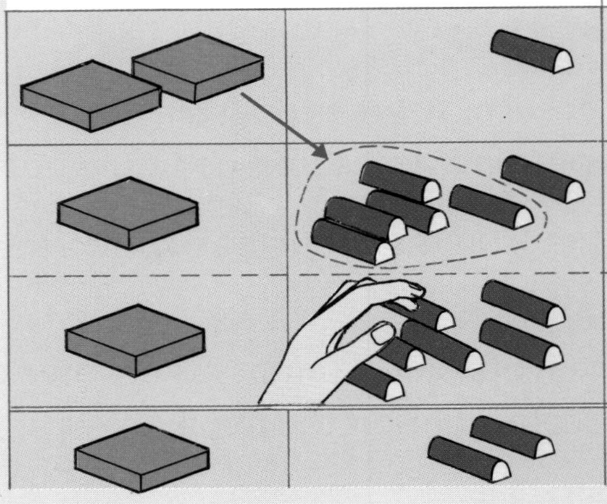

		boxes	bars
		2	1
		1	6
		—	4
		1	2

1 Set out 5-rods (or base 5 longs) for boxes and units for choc-bars to do these "take away" problems for Mr Sweet.
The first one is done for you with a picture.

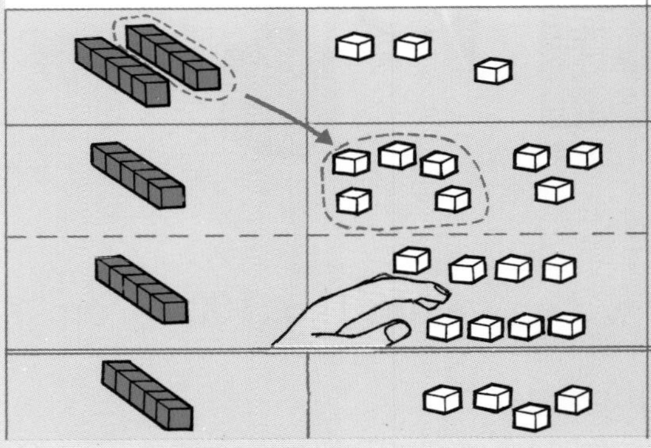

		boxes	bars
		2	3
		1	8
		—	4
		1	4

a

boxes	bars
2	3
—	4
1	4

b

boxes	bars
3	1
—	2

c

boxes	bars
4	2
— 1	3

d

boxes	bars
2	0
—	4

e

boxes	bars
3	3
— 2	4

Grouping in sixes: subtraction

Mrs Giles wanted 5 eggs to make a cake. She had 2 boxes and 3 eggs.

I want to take away 5 eggs so I must open up a box. Now I have 1 box and 9 eggs. I can take away 5 eggs. That leaves 1 box and 4 eggs.

		boxes	eggs
	○ ○○	2	3
	○○○ ○○○ ○○○	1	9
	○○○○ ○○○	—	5
	○○○○	1	4

1 Set out 6-rods for boxes (or base 6 longs) and units for eggs to do these "take away" problems for Mrs Giles.

a	boxes	eggs	**b**	boxes	eggs	**c**	boxes	eggs	**d**	boxes	eggs
	2	4		3	2		4	1		3	0
−		5	−		4	−	2	3	−	1	5

Using the multi-base board for subtraction

John is using squares, longs and units on the base 4 set.

A long is made from 4 units.

A square is made from 4 longs.

He sets these out on the multi-base board.

He takes away 1 long and 2 units.

This is the answer.

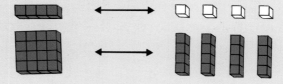

squares	longs	units		He records: S L U
				1 3 3
				− 1 2
				1 2 1

How could John do this one?

```
S L U
1 2 1
—     3
_____
```

Set out the pieces and see if you can do it.
(Remember how Mr Sweet and Mrs Giles
did their 'take away' problems.)

He records:

John wants to take
away 3 units.

There are not enough
units, so he changes
1 long for 4 units.

Now he can take away
3 units.

This is the answer.

squares	longs	units

```
S L U

1 2 1


1 1 5


—     3
_____

1 1 2
_____
```

1 Use a multi-base board with squares, longs and units (base 4) to do these:

a
```
S L U
2 2 3
—   1 1
_____
```

c
```
S L U
1 1 2
—     3
_____
```

e
```
S L U
3 3 1
—   2 2
_____
```

g
```
S L U
2 2 3
—   3 1
_____
```

b
```
S L U
1 3 2
—   1 3
_____
```

d
```
S L U
2 3 2
—   2 3
_____
```

f
```
S L U
2 2 2
—   3 3
_____
```

h
```
S L U
2 0 0
—   1 2
_____
```

In base five

A long is made from 5 units.

A square is made from 5 longs.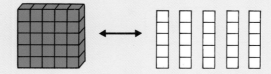

1 Use a multi-base board, squares, long and units (base 5) for these:

	a S L U		**b** S L U		**c** S L U		**d** S L U
	1 4 1		2 3 3		2 4 2		2 2 4
	− 3		− 4		− 2 4		− 3 1

In base ten

A long is made from 10 units.

A square is made from 10 longs.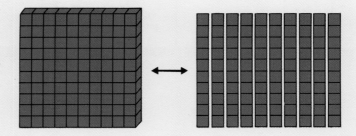

2 Use a multi-base board and squares, long and units in the base 10 set.

a S L U	**c** S L U	**e** S L U	**g** S L U
7 4	3 4	6 0	2 3 2
− 3 2	− 1 8	− 2 4	− 4 7

b S L U	**d** S L U	**f** S L U	**h** S L U
3 2 7	1 1 1	4 2 4	4 0 0
− 4 3	− 5 5	−2 6 5	−2 3 6

Subtraction on the abacus

For example: 17—4.

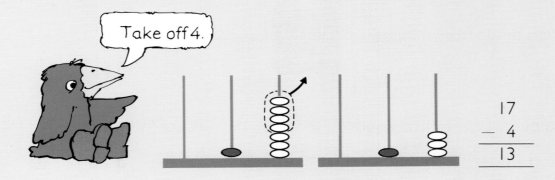

This is how 23—6 is done on the abacus.

Start with 23.   Not enough units to take off 6, so exchange a "ten" bead for ten units.   Take away 6.   Put the other 4 with the 3 units. This leaves 17.

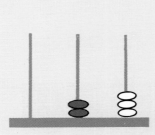 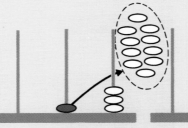 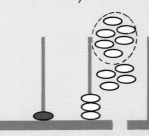

$$\begin{array}{r} 23 \\ -\ 6 \\ \hline 17 \end{array}$$

1 Use your abacus to do these subtractions.
Draw an abacus picture in your answer when you write it in your book.

a	19—6	**e**	44—1 ten	**i**	thirty-one—2	**m**	61—eleven
b	27—5	**f**	35—twenty	**j**	fifty-six—16	**n**	70—5 tens
c	20—1	**g**	46—33	**k**	19—eleven	**o**	11—1
d	24—6	**h**	48—twenty-four	**l**	90—eleven	**p**	76—67

2 Take 10 from each of these numbers:

a 17   **b** 19   **c** 30   **d** 51   **e** 36   **f** ninety   **g** 88   **h** 10

Chapter 10: Subtraction 1

Subtracting tens and units

1 Do these subtraction problems in your book.
Remember to estimate first by rounding numbers to the nearest 10.

a 46
   −25

b 37
   −13

c 88
   −34

d 65
   −44

e 99
   −73

Splitting tens

Sometimes there are not enough units in the top number,
so a ten has to be exchanged for 10 units.

Mary has 32p and John has no money. Mary wants to give 17p to John.

There are not
enough 🪙 coins.

She changes
1 🪙 coin for
10 🪙 coins.

She gives 17p
to John.

She has 15p left.

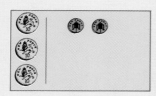

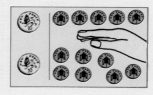

$$(30+2) \longrightarrow (20+12) \longrightarrow (20+12)$$
$$\underline{-(10+\ 7)}$$
$$(10+\ 5) \longrightarrow 15p$$

Using ten-rods and units, the problem looks like this:
Start with 32.   There are not enough
                    units, so exchange
                    1 rod for 10 units.   Take away 17.   15 are left.

$$(30+2) \longrightarrow (20+12) \longrightarrow (20+12)$$
$$\underline{-(10+\ 7)}$$
$$(10+\ 5) \longrightarrow 15$$

Use ten-rods and units like this for 53 − 26.

Start with 53.

There are not enough units, so exchange 1 rod for 10 units.

Take away 26.

27 are left.

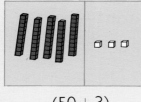

$(50 + 3)$

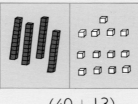

$(40 + 13)$

$$\begin{array}{r} (40 + 13) \\ -(20 + \ 6) \\ \hline (20 + \ 7) \end{array}$$

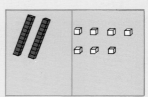

$= \quad 27$

Remember — estimate, calculate, check.

1 Now try these. Set them out in the same way.

a 36 −19	**b** 75 −48	**c** 64 −29	**d** 50 −17	**e** 44 −35	**f** 52 − 9

Here is a shorter way of setting out:

$$\begin{array}{r} 53 \\ -29 \\ \hline \end{array}$$

There are not enough units so exchange a 10.
50 + 3 becomes 40 + 13.

$$\begin{array}{r} {}^{4}\ {}^{13} \\ \not5\ \not3 \\ -2\ 9 \\ \hline 2\ 4 \end{array}$$

2 These have been started for you. Copy and complete.

a	b	c	d	e	f
⁴ ¹³ $\not5\ \not3$ −1 7	² ¹⁶ $\not3\ \not6$ −1 9	⁸ ¹² $\not9\ \not2$ −6 5	⁵ ¹⁶ $\not6\ \not6$ −3 9	⁴ ¹⁰ $\not5\ \not0$ −2 2	⁷ ¹³ $\not8\ \not3$ −1 9

3 Try these. Set them out in the same way.

a 53 −18	**c** 86 −37	**e** 55 −26	**g** 80 −36	**i** 73 −47	**k** 73 −65
b 72 −49	**d** 67 −48	**f** 70 −52	**h** 73 −38	**j** 73 −56	**l** 47 −28

Subtracting hundreds, tens and units

Start with 256.   Take away 124.

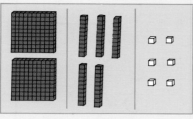   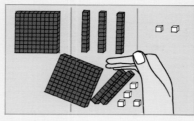   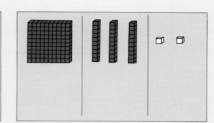

200 + 50 + 6 ⟶ (200 + 50 + 6)
　　　　　　　　　−(100 + 20 + 4)
　　　　　　　　　　100 + 30 + 2　　　=　　　132

1 Copy and complete:

a 275　　(200 +　　+　　)　　　　**b** 366　　(300 +　　+　　)
　−143　−(100 + 40 + 3)　　　　　− 52　−(　　50 + 2)
　　　　　　100 +　　+　　=　　　　　　　　　　　　+　　+　　=

2 Remember to estimate first by rounding numbers to the nearest 100. Set these out the same way:

a 456　　**b** 477　　**c** 327　　**d** 188　　**e** 453　　**f** 580
　−234　　　− 73　　　−117　　　− 60　　　−320　　　−310

Splitting tens again

265 − 137

Start with 265.

There are not enough units so exchange a ten for 10 units.

Take away 137.

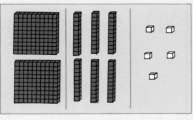   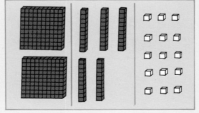   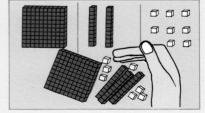

200 + 60 + 5 ⟶ 200 + 50 + 15 ⟶ (200 + 50 + 15)
　　　　　　　　　　　　　　　　　−(100 + 30 + 7)
　　　　　　　　　　　　　　　　　　100 + 20 + 8 = 128

1 Use squares, ten-rods and units.
Copy and complete.

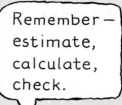

a 273 ⟶ (200+70+3) ⟶ (200+ 60 +   )
  −146 ⟶ (100+40+6) ⟶ (100+ 40 + 6)
  ⟵ (100+   +   )

b 281 ⟶ (200+80+1) ⟶ (200+   +   )
  − 67 ⟶ −(60+7) ⟶ −(60 + 7)
  ⟵ (200+   +   )

2 Set these out in the same way.

a 341	**b** 176	**c** 322	**d** 460	**e** 385	**f** 743
−138	− 49	−108	− 36	−179	−534

Now try the shorter way:

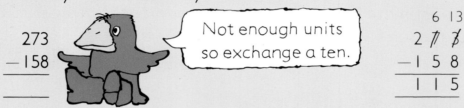

273
−158
——

Not enough units so exchange a ten.

  6 13
2 7̶ 3̶
−1 5 8
———
1 1 5

3 These have been started for you. Copy and complete.

	4 14		6 12		5 10		2 15		1 17		2 13
a	2 8̶ 4̶	**b**	5 7̶ 2̶	**c**	8 6̶ 0̶	**d**	4 3̶ 5̶	**e**	3 7̶ 7̶	**f**	5 8̶ 3̶
	−1 2 9		−3 4 6		−3 2 4		−1 0 8		−1 1 9		− 5 1 7

4 Set these out the shortest way:

a 342	**c** 760	**e** 873	**g** 217	**i** 550	**k** 241
−125	−232	− 59	−108	− 27	−109

b 492	**d** 342	**f** 470	**h** 635	**j** 740	**l** 753
− 47	−136	−436	−219	−332	−246

Chapter 11: Weight 1

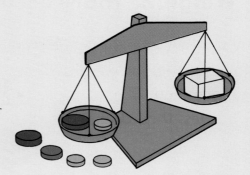

Using smaller weights

You often need to use several different sizes of weight together to balance something.

1 What do these weights add up to? Copy and complete.

   a 10g + 10g + 10g = □ g   **d** 20g + 20g + 20g + 10g = □ g

   b 20g + 10g + 10g = □ g   **e** 50g + 10g + 10g + 10g = □ g

   c 20g + 20g + 20g = □ g   **f** 50g + 20g + 10g = □ g

2 Copy and complete this table showing how to make different totals using 50g, 20g and 10g weights.

	50g	20g	10g	total
a	1	1	1	80 g
b	0	1	1	□ g
c	1	1	0	□ g
d	0	1	2	□ g

	50g	20g	10g	total
e	1	0	1	□ g
f	1	2	1	□ g
g	1	0	3	□ g
h	0	3	2	□ g

3 Now weigh some real things using different sized weights as you need them.
Estimate the weight first and record like this:

object	estimate	weight
book	□ g	□ g
cup	□ g	□ g

4 There are lots of ways of making smaller weights add up to 100g. Copy and complete:

   a 60g + □ g = 100g   **c** 30g + □ g = 100g

   b □ g + 50g = 100g   **d** 20g + 20g + □ g = 100g

5 Now try subtracting weights. Copy and complete.

   a 100g − 40g = □ g   **c** 100g − 30g = □ g

   b 100g − □ g = 20g   **d** □ g − 50g = 50g

Weighing more accurately

Using 100g weights,
we find a book weighs
more than 100g
but less than 200g.

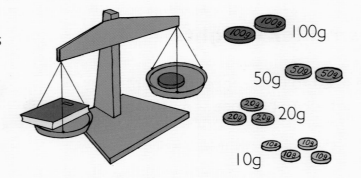

100g

50g

20g

10g

Start with a 100g weight then add a 50g weight.
If the book still does not balance add smaller
weights till the book balances. Keep counting the
total weight as you go; this is called 'counting on'.

Steps

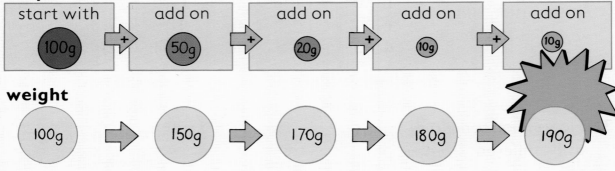

total correct
weight of book.

I Practise counting on with these examples.
Write down the total weight after each step.
The first one is done for you in full, complete the others in the same way.

a Steps 100g + 50g + 10g + 10g
Weight 100g → 150g → 160g → 170g total

b 100g + 50g + 20g + 10g

c 100g + 20g + 20g + 10g + 10g

d 100g + 50g + 10g + 10g + 10g

e 100g + 20g + 10g + 10g

f 100g + 100g + 20g + 20g

g 100g + 100g + 100g + 50g + 10g

h 100g + 100g + 50g + 20g

i 100g + 100g + 20g + 10g

Suppose you have a panful of jumbled weights to count.
Pick out the heaviest first then the next heaviest
and count on till you reach the total.

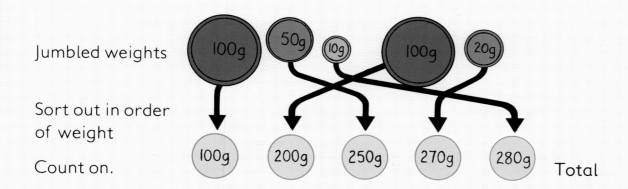

Jumbled weights

Sort out in order
of weight

Count on.   Total

I   Copy these jumbles into your book and
    sort them out in the same way.

a

b

c

d

e   This one is recorded as
    1 kg and □ g.

Weighing in kilograms and grams

2   Use the scales to weigh some things that you think weigh about 1 kg.
    Estimate the weight first.
    Record the estimates and correct weights in a table like this:

object	estimate kg	g	weight kg	g
dictionary	1	200	0	970
bottle	0	750	1	40
and so on. . . .				

Chapter 12: Subtraction 2

Splitting hundreds

This time, token cards are used to show: $324 - 152$

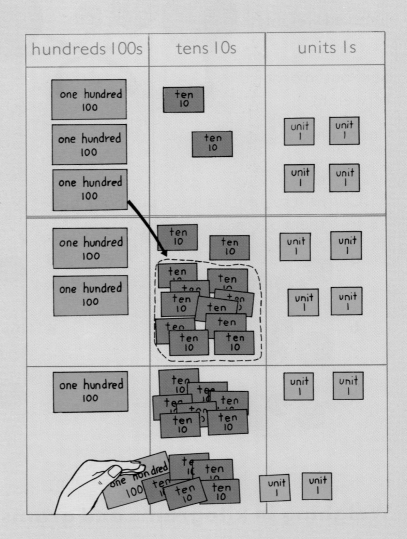

Start with 324:

3 100 s + 2 10 s + 4 1 s

To take away 152:

1 100 + 5 10 s + 2 1 s
there are enough 1 s
but not enough 10 s.

Exchange a 100 token
for ten 10 s.

3 100 s + 2 10 s + 4 1 s

2 100 s + 12 10 s + 4 1 s

Take away
(1 100 + 5 10 + 2 1)

Record like this:

$$
\begin{array}{r}
324 \longrightarrow (200 + 120 + 4) \\
-152 \longrightarrow -(100 + 50 + 2) \\
\hline
172 \longleftarrow (100 + 70 + 2)
\end{array}
$$

1 Remember to estimate first by rounding numbers to the nearest 100.
Use squares, longs and units or token cards for these.
Set them out in the same way.

a 346 − 180	**c** 408 − 276	**e** 525 − 281	**g** 308 − 124
b 210 − 90	**d** 520 − 218	**f** 216 − 170	**h** 672 − 492

The shorter way of setting out can be used:

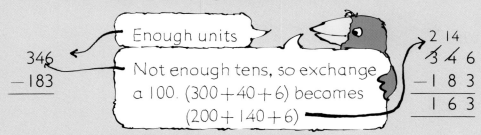

```
346
-183
```

```
  2 14
  3 4 6
-1 8 3
  1 6 3
```

1 Remember — estimate, calculate, check.
These have been started for you. Copy and complete.

```
    1 12          7 10          8 11          2 10          6 10
a   2 2 0    c    8 6 0    e    9 1 8    g    3 6 7    i    7 6 8
  -   8 0       -3 9 0        -2 7 0        -1 7 6        -5 8 8
```

```
    3 13          3 12          6 18          3 12          7 17
b   4 3 0    d    4 2 4    f    7 8 2    h    4 2 6    j    8 7 5
  -1 7 0        -2 8 3        -  9 0        -1 5 6        -3 8 2
```

2 Try these. Set them out in the same way:

a	430	**c**	876	**e**	752	**g**	363	**i**	308	**k**	429
	− 60		−492		−280		−281		−238		−218
b	281	**d**	500	**f**	907	**h**	405	**j**	666	**l**	728
	−190		−330		−645		−265		−484		−688

3 Read these carefully. Make sure you know which number
to start with and which number to subtract.

a From 283 take 191.

b Take 384 from 509.

c A farmer picks 748kg of apples.
If he sells 560kg how many kg are left?

d By how many is 600 greater than 280?

e 882 is less than 909 by how many?

f Subtract 186 from 306.

g John had 205 stamps but gave away 92. How many were left?

h Anne needs 315 points to win a game. She scores 175.
How many more points does she need?

Splitting hundreds and tens

Look at these pictures
for 223 — 45.

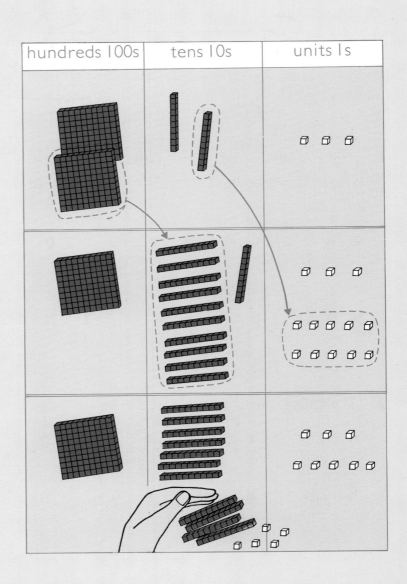

hundreds 100s	tens 10s	units 1s

Start with 223.
  2 (100)+2 (10)+3 (1)

To take away 45:
  4 (10)+5 (1)
there are not enough 1's
and not enough 10s.

Exchange a 10 rod for
10 units and a 100 square
for ten 10-rods.

Now you can
take away 45.

Record like this:

223 $\longrightarrow$ (200+ 10+13) $\longrightarrow$ (100+110+13)
− 45 $\longrightarrow$ − (40+ 5) $\longrightarrow$ −(40+ 5)
178 $\longleftarrow$ (100+ 70+ 8)

I Remember — estimate, calculate, check.
  Use squares, longs and units or token cards for these:

  a 334—57   **c** 355—168   **e** 846—288   **g** 645—456
  b 245—79   **d** 260—186   **f** 552—85   **h** 200—38

The last question **h** is a little different because when you tried
to exchange a ten there weren't any tens. What did you do?

For 200 – 38:

Start with 200.
There are not enough units
or tens to take away 38.
First exchange a 100 for
ten 10-rods.

Then exchange a ten-rod
for ten units.
Record like this:

$$
\begin{array}{ll}
200 & (100+90+10) \\
-\ 38 & -\quad\ (30+\ 8) \\
\hline
162 & (100+60+\ 2)
\end{array}
$$

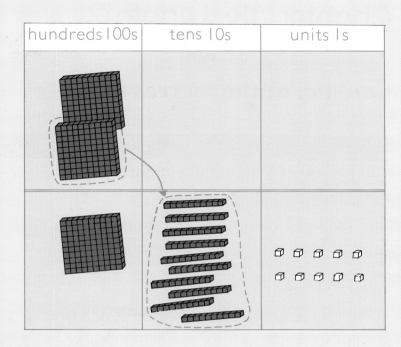

hundreds 100s	tens 10s	units 1s

Here is the shorter way of setting out when hundreds
and tens have to be split.

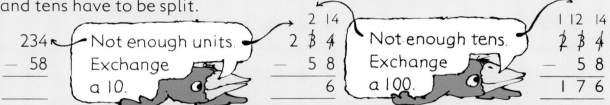

$$
\begin{array}{r}
234 \\
-\ 58 \\
\hline
\end{array}
\qquad
\begin{array}{r}
^{2\ \ 14} \\
2\ \cancel{3}\ 4 \\
-\ 5\ 8 \\
\hline
6 \\
\end{array}
\qquad
\begin{array}{r}
^{1\ 12\ 14} \\
\cancel{2}\ \cancel{3}\ 4 \\
-\quad 5\ 8 \\
\hline
1\ 7\ 6 \\
\end{array}
$$

Not enough units.
Exchange a 10.

Not enough tens.
Exchange a 100.

1 Remember — estimate, calculate, check.
These have been started for you. Copy and complete.

$$
\begin{array}{cccccc}
\mathbf{a}\ \overset{2\ 11\ 16}{\cancel{3}\cancel{2}\cancel{6}} &
\mathbf{b}\ \overset{3\ 13\ 14}{\cancel{4}\cancel{4}\cancel{4}} &
\mathbf{c}\ \overset{4\ 14\ 15}{\cancel{5}\cancel{5}\cancel{5}} &
\mathbf{d}\ \overset{2\ 11\ 14}{\cancel{3}\cancel{2}\cancel{4}} &
\mathbf{e}\ \overset{4\ 15\ 13}{\cancel{5}\cancel{6}\cancel{3}} &
\mathbf{f}\ \overset{2\ 9\ 10}{\cancel{3}\cancel{0}\cancel{0}} \\
-\ \ 4\ 8 & -1\ 5\ 6 & -2\ 7\ 9 & -1\ 8\ 8 & -\ \ 9\ 5 & -1\ 7\ 6
\end{array}
$$

2 Try these. Set them out the same way.

a 325	**b** 666	**c** 111	**d** 216	**e** 742	**f** 700
– 49	–278	– 43	–147	– 55	–444

3 Set out each subtraction carefully, then copy and complete
the computer tape.

– 156	500	400	300	200	246	354	462	570	678

4 Write some short number stories which lead to subtraction problems.

Chapter 13: Length 2

Looking at the metre ruler

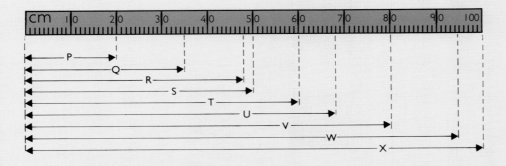

1 Write down the letter for each arrow and its length.
For example: Line P is 20 cm long.

2 Work out the total length of these lines.

    a P and Q   **c** P and V   **e** Q and T   **g** P and T
    b P and S   **d** Q and S   **f** R and T   **h** U and R

The metre, decimetre and centimetre

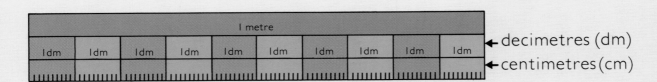

3 Copy and complete:

    a There are ☐ cm in 1 decimetre   **d** There are ☐ cm in 10 decimetres
    b There are ☐ cm in 2 decimetres   **e** There are ☐ decimetres in 1 metre
    c There are ☐ cm in 5 decimetres   **f** There are ☐ cm in one metre

Because there are ten decimetres in one metre, 1 decimetre is a tenth of a metre $1\,dm = \frac{1}{10}m$	Because there are 100 centimetres in one metre, 1 centimetre is a hundredth of a metre $1\,cm = \frac{1}{100}m$

Recording measurements on a decimal abacus

These columns record the number of **whole** metres.

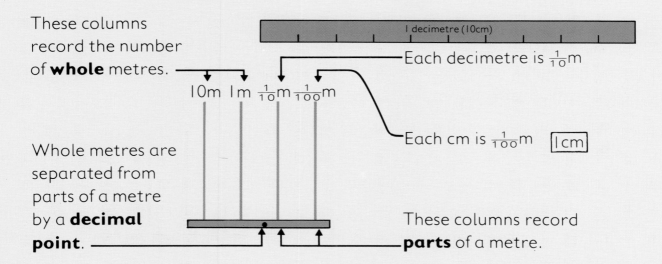

Each decimetre is $\frac{1}{10}$m

10m 1m $\frac{1}{10}$m $\frac{1}{100}$m

Each cm is $\frac{1}{100}$m   1cm

Whole metres are separated from parts of a metre by a **decimal point**.

These columns record **parts** of a metre.

This is how 16cm is recorded on the abacus:

16cm = 10cm + 6cm
     = $\frac{1}{10}$m + $\frac{6}{100}$m

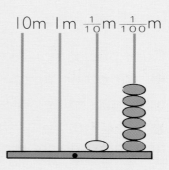

10m 1m $\frac{1}{10}$m $\frac{1}{100}$m

1 Record these in the same way with abacus pictures.

a 14cm	**c** 28cm	**e** 30cm	**g** 99cm
b 23cm	**d** 29cm	**f** 45cm	**h** 100cm

2 Copy and complete.

a 100cm = □ m	**d** 3m = □ cm	**g** 1000cm = □ m	**j** 11m = □ cm
b 200cm = □ m	**e** 7m = □ cm	**h** 1200cm = □ m	**k** 13m = □ cm
c 400cm = □ m	**f** 9m = □ cm	**i** 3500cm = □ m	**l** 17m = □ cm

This is how 214cm can be recorded on an abacus:

214cm = 200cm + 10cm + 4cm
      = 2m + $\frac{1}{10}$m + $\frac{4}{100}$m = 2.14m

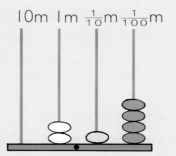

10m 1m $\frac{1}{10}$m $\frac{1}{100}$m

3 Draw an abacus picture for each of these measurements.

a 316cm   **b** 124cm   **c** 653cm   **d** 302cm   **e** 1440cm   **f** 1030cm

I A builder used a metre stick and a decimetre strip
to measure lengths of wood.

He recorded the lengths in two ways —

like this: and like this:

	m	dm	cm
a	2	1	8
b	6	3	2
c	9	4	6
d	7	5	8
e	1	9	1
f	15	6	0

m	cm
2	18

Here is
measurement **a**
shown on an abacus.

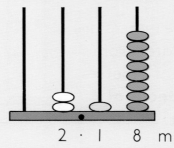

2 · 1   8   m

2m 18cm or 2·18m

Copy and complete the second table and draw abacus pictures
for the other measurements.

2 Write the measurements shown by these abacus pictures,
first in m and cm then using a decimal point.
For example: **a** 13m 23cm   13·23m

a

10m 1m $\frac{1}{10}$m $\frac{1}{100}$m

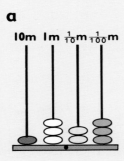

b

10m 1m $\frac{1}{10}$m $\frac{1}{100}$m

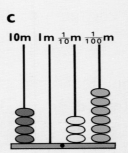

c

10m 1m $\frac{1}{10}$m $\frac{1}{100}$m

d

10m 1m $\frac{1}{10}$m $\frac{1}{100}$m

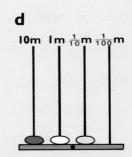

3 Record measurements made in your classroom.
Draw decimal abacus pictures of your results.

object or distance	whole metres	parts of a metre(cm)	metres and parts together
height of a door	1	98	1·98m
width of door			
distance of my desk from door			
height of my friend			

Finding the perimeter

Remember to estimate first by rounding to the nearest 10cm.

To find the perimeter of this shape add the lengths of the sides together:

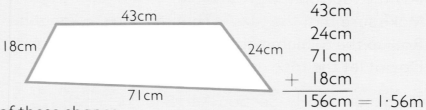

```
  43cm
  24cm
  71cm
+ 18cm
───────
 156cm = 1·56m
```

1 Find the perimeter of these shapes.

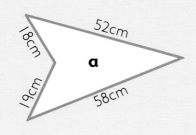

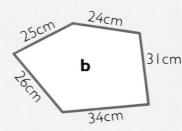

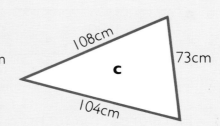

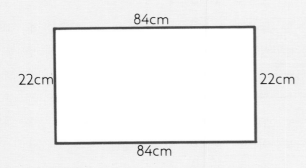

Opposite sides of a rectangle are the same length, so the perimeter can be worked out like this:

2 (84cm) + 2 (22cm)

```
 168cm
+ 44cm
────────
 212cm = 2·12m
```

2 Find the perimeters of these rectangles.

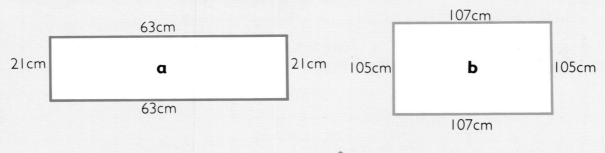

e What is the quick way of working out the perimeter of a square?

3 Find the perimeter of six things in your classroom and record your results.

Using a measuring tape

Always work with a partner.
Lay the tape on the ground and do not let it sag.
Make sure that the tape is running in a straight line.
Roll up the tape immediately after each measurement.
Do not let the tape get wet or muddy.

If we look closely, Section A to B looks like this:

1   Here are some sections taken from a measuring tape.
Read off and record the measurements shown by the arrows.

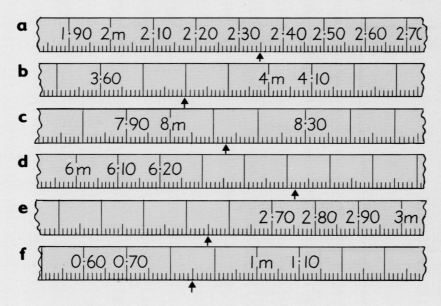

2   Use your tape measure to measure and record like this:

	whole metres	decimetre sections	cm over	total m
width of your classroom		•		•
length of a wall		•		•
length of playground		•		•
distance from window to door		•		•

Chapter 14: Multiplication 1

Square numbers up to 100

You have met
the first six
square numbers.

$1 \times 1 = 1$ $2 \times 2 = 4$ $3 \times 3 = 9$ $4 \times 4 = 16$ $5 \times 5 = 25$ $6 \times 6 = 36$

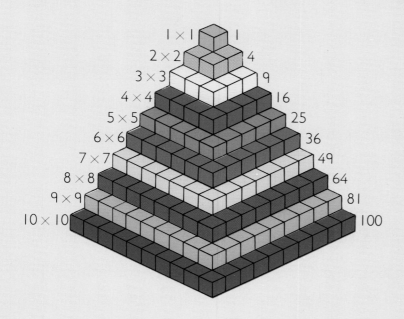

1×1 1
2×2 4
3×3 9
4×4 16
5×5 25
6×6 36
7×7 49
8×8 64
9×9 81
10×10 100

This diagram shows
the square numbers
up to 100.

Learn these ten
square numbers.

1 Square numbers   1   4   9   16   ☐   36   ☐   64   ☐   100
   Differences   3   5   ○   9   11   ○   15   ○   19

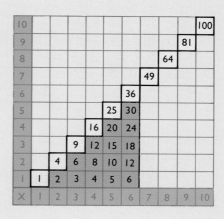

The square numbers make a diagonal on
the 10×10 multiplication square.
$5 \times 3 = 3 \times 5$, etc. so
we only need to fill in
one side of the diagonal.
You should know the products in **"Zone A"**,
which is shaded.

2   Cover the table square then copy and complete.
   a $4 \times 4 = $ ☐   **d** $2 \times 2 = $ ☐   **g** $4 \times 6 = $ ☐   **j** $6 \times 3 = $ ☐   **m** $5 \times $ ☐ $= 20$
   b $5 \times 3 = $ ☐   **e** $5 \times 5 = $ ☐   **h** $7 \times 7 = $ ☐   **k** $9 \times 9 = $ ☐   **n** $8 \times $ ☐ $= 64$
   c $2 \times 6 = $ ☐   **f** $4 \times 3 = $ ☐   **i** $3 \times 6 = $ ☐   **l** $6 \times 1 = $ ☐   **o** $6 \times $ ☐ $= 36$

The next products to be learned are in **Zone B.**

The table of 1's is easy. Any number multiplied by 1 is itself.

Doubling gives the rest of the table of 2's: 14, 16, 18, 20.

The 10's table is easy too: 10, 20, 30, 40, 50, 60, 70, 80, 90

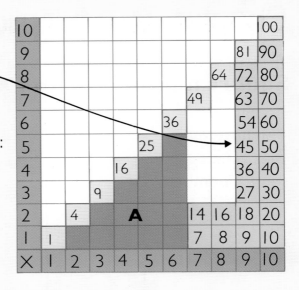

The 9's table has a clear pattern.

$9 \times 1 = 9$ $0+9=9$
$9 \times 2 = 18$ $1+8=9$
$9 \times 3 = 27$ $2+7=9$
$9 \times 4 = 36$ $3+6=9$
$9 \times 5 = 45$ $4+5=9$
$9 \times 6 = 54$ $5+4=9$
$9 \times 7 = 63$ $6+3=9$
$9 \times 8 = 72$ $7+2=9$
$9 \times 9 = 81$ $8+1=9$
$9 \times 10 = 90$ $9+0=9$

The digits in the product add up to 9. From each product to the next is "10 up and 1 down". ($+10-1$ is the same as $+9$)

The number of tens is 1 less than the number you are multiplying the 9 by.

For example: $9 \times 3 = 2\square$ "Twenty-something"
$2+7=9$ so $9 \times 3 = 27$

$9 \times 6 = 5\square$ "Fifty-something"
$5+4=9$ so $9 \times 6 = 54$

I   Cover Zone B of the table and try these:

a $2 \times 8 = \square$ **c** $10 \times 7 = \square$ **e** $9 \times 4 = \square$ **g** $9 \times \square = 72$ **i** $10 \times \square = 40$

b $9 \times 1 = \square$ **d** $9 \times 10 = \square$ **f** $9 \times 7 = \square$ **h** $9 \times \square = 81$ **j** $\square \times 10 = 80$

The 9's table can be shown on your fingers. For $9 \times \mathbf{4}$, turn down the **4**th finger from the left. These show the number of tens (3).

These show the numbers of units (6).

$30 + 6 = 36$
$9 \times 4 = 36$

Try it for the rest of the 9's table.

Zone C has only nine products to learn.

Two of these are part of the easy
5's table.
5, 10, 15, 20, 25, 30, 35, 40, 45, 50.

Two are "double doubles".
$7 \times 4 = 7 \times 2 \times 2 = 14 \times 2 = 28$
$8 \times 4 = 8 \times 2 \times 2 = 32$

The 8's table is "double 4's".
$8 \times 3 = 2(4 \times 3) = 2(12) = 24$
$8 \times 4 = 2(4 \times 4) = 2(16) = 32$
$8 \times 6 = 2(4 \times 6) = 2(24) = 48$
$8 \times 7 = 2(4 \times 7) = 2(28) = 56$

and $7 \times 6 = 2(7 \times 3) = 2(21) = 42$

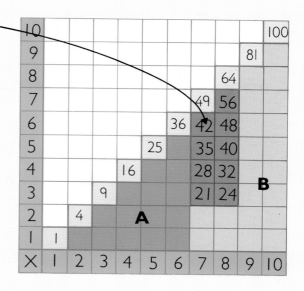

I Cover Zone C and try these:

a $7 \times 3 = \square$ **c** $6 \times 8 = \square$ **e** $8 \times 4 = \square$ **g** $5 \times 7 = \square$ **i** $8 \times \square = 56$

b $5 \times 8 = \square$ **d** $7 \times 6 = \square$ **f** $7 \times 8 = \square$ **h** $7 \times 4 = \square$ **j** $7 \times \square = 42$

2 On squared paper, make a
multiplication square. Fill the
square numbers and Zones A, B, C.
Now make a table jig-saw by
cutting along the lines. See if your
friend can fit it together again.

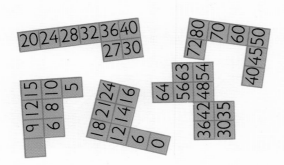

3 Use 100 square number grids to
mark table patterns in colour. The
picture shows the 7's pattern.

1	2	3	4	5	6	7	8	9	10
11	12	13	14	15	16	17	18	19	20
21	22	23	24	25	26	27	28	29	30
31	32	33	34	35	36	37	38	39	40
41	42	43	44	45	46	47	48	49	50
51	52	53	54	55	56	57	58	59	60

4 When you know your tables, multiplying 20, 30, 40, . . . etc.
by units is easy: $30 \times 4 = 3 \times 4 \times 10 = 12 \times 10 = 120$

Try these: **a** $20 \times 4 = \square$ **c** $60 \times 3 = \square$ **e** $80 \times 9 = \square$ **g** $50 \times 6 = \square$

b $30 \times 5 = \square$ **d** $40 \times 7 = \square$ **f** $9 \times 30 = \square$ **h** $8 \times 80 = \square$

Chapter 15: Area

Counting square centimetres

Square units are counted to find the **area** of a surface.
A square with sides of one centimetre has an area of **one square centimetre**.

The area of this rectangle is 6 square centimetres.
To save writing square centimetre in full every time it is
needed, cm² can be written and read as "square centimetre".

1 What is the area, in cm², of these rectangles?

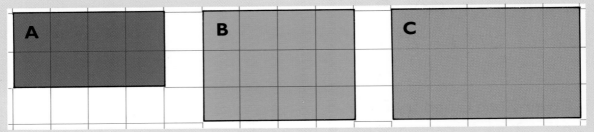

2 It is easy to work out the area of a shape which is half of a rectangle.
Write down the area of these.

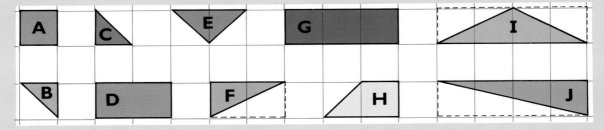

3 Now work out these areas in cm².

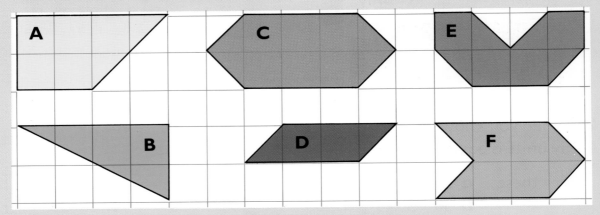

I Using paper marked in cm², draw shapes which have the following areas :
   a 6 cm²   **b** 10 cm²   **c** 15 cm²   **d** 21 cm²   **e** 19 cm²

2 **a** Draw a rectangle with the same area as the triangle.
   b Draw a square with the same area as the rectangle.

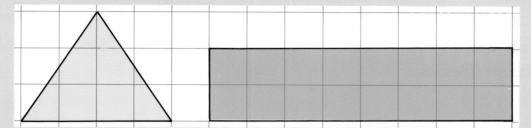

3 On a piece of tracing paper, trace
the grid from some one-centimetre
squared paper. The traced grid can
be used to find the area of a surface
by putting it over and counting
the squares.

Use the squared tracing paper to
find the areas of surfaces such
as the front cover of a book
or the top of a small box.

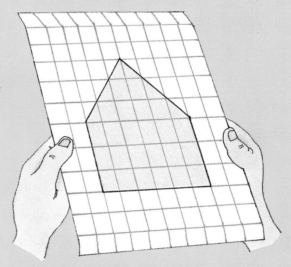

Record in your book like this : The reading book has an area of 300 cm².

Irregular shapes

If we put the tracing paper over
a shape like this or copy the shape
on to squared paper it does not
fit exactly on to grid squares.

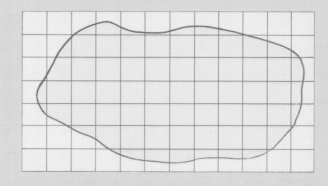

To find its approximate
area, count:
24   whole squares (✗)
 9   pieces of ½ or more
—   of a square (✓)
33 cm² approximately.

Count as a square if it is
more than half.
Do not count if less than
half.

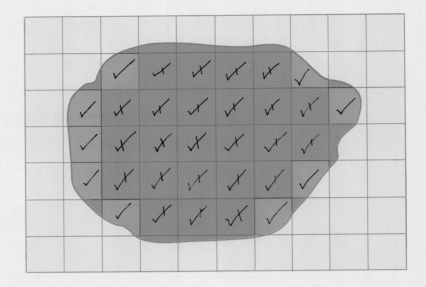

1 a Estimate the area, in cm²,
of this shape.
b Copy the shape onto a grid of
square centimetres.
c Find its approximate area by
counting the squares.
d How many cm² different was
your estimate?

2 Place your hand flat with
fingers together on a piece of
centimetre squared paper.
Draw round your hand and
find its approximate area.

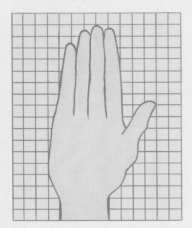

3

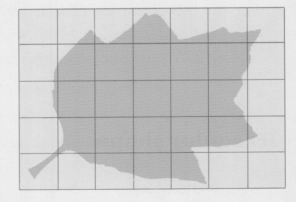

Find the approximate area of
this leaf in cm². Make a collection
of leaves from different trees.
Sort them into order of their
areas, starting with the smallest.

Working out areas

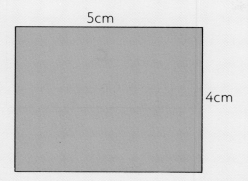

5cm

4cm

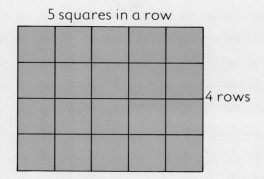

5 squares in a row

4 rows

This rectangle is 5cm long and 4cm wide.

If it is covered with square centimetres there are 5 squares in a row and 4 rows.
The area of the rectangle is 20cm².

If you know the number of squares in a row, and the number of rows, how can you find the number of squares in the area?

I What is the area of each of these rectangles drawn on a centimetre square grid? Record like this: A is 10cm².

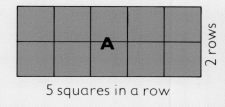

A

5 squares in a row

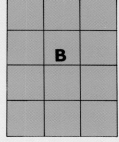

B

2 rows

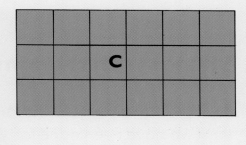

C

2 Find the areas of these rectangles and record.

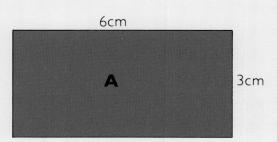

6cm

A

3cm

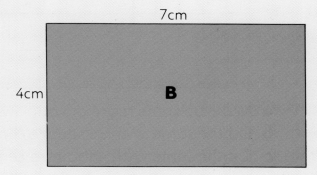

7cm

4cm

B

I Measure the sides of these rectangles and then find their areas.

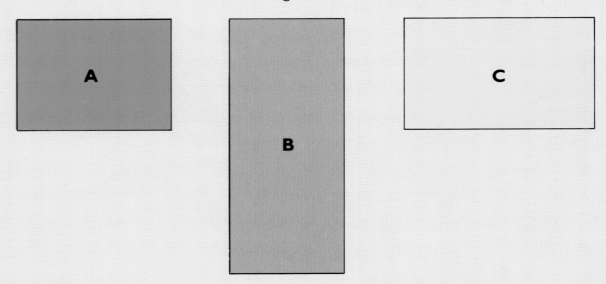

2 Find the areas of these shapes which are made from rectangles.

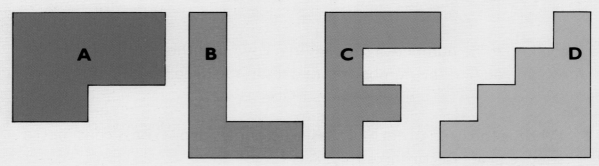

Shapes with the same area

3 You can arrange 24 square centimetres to form different rectangles. Two have been done for you.

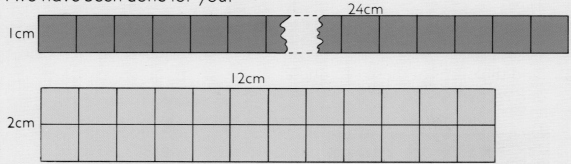

    a Make up some more of your own using 24 square centimetres.

    b Do the same with 36 square centimetres.

    c Do the same with 48 square centimetres.

Chapter 16: Division 1

Checking division on the multiplication square

For $42 \div 7 = \square$, go along the 7 row until you reach 42. 42 is in the 6 column so $42 \div 7 = 6$ because $7 \times 6 = 42$.

10	10	20	30	40	50	60	70	80	90	100
9	9	18	27	36	45	54	63	72	81	90
8	8	16	24	32	40	48	56	64	72	80
7	7	14	21	28	35	42	49	56	63	70
6	6	12	18	24	30	36	42	48	54	60
5	5	10	15	20	25	30	35	40	45	50
4	4	8	12	16	20	24	28	32	36	40
3	3	6	9	12	15	18	21	24	27	30
2	2	4	6	8	10	12	14	16	18	20
1	1	2	3	4	5	6	7	8	9	10
×	1	2	3	4	5	6	7	8	9	10

1 Cover the multiplication square but use it to check your answers **after** copying and completing these:

a $35 \div 7 = \square$ f $45 \div 5 = \square$

b $36 \div 4 = \square$ g $27 \div 3 = \square$

c $18 \div 2 = \square$ h $32 \div 8 = \square$

d $27 \div 9 = \square$ i $54 \div 6 = \square$

e $56 \div 8 = \square$ j $72 \div 8 = \square$

2 a

$\div 6$	6	42	30	18	48	60	54	36

c

$\div 8$	40	80	32	16	64	48	24	56

b

$\div 7$	14	21	7	63	49	42	70	56

d

$\div 9$	18	81	27	72	36	63	45	54

Here is another way to set out division:
"36 divided by 4 is $\square$"
or "How many sets of 4 are contained in 36?"

$$4 \overline{)36}^{\,9}$$

The answer goes above the number you are dividing.

3 Copy and complete:

a $4 \overline{)24}^{\square}$ d $6 \overline{)48}^{\square}$ g $10 \overline{)60}^{\square}$ j $6 \overline{)42}^{\square}$ m $8 \overline{)56}^{\square}$ p $8 \overline{)48}^{\square}$

b $6 \overline{)54}^{\square}$ e $2 \overline{)16}^{\square}$ h $7 \overline{)49}^{\square}$ k $5 \overline{)35}^{\square}$ n $10 \overline{)90}^{\square}$ q $7 \overline{)63}^{\square}$

c $5 \overline{)40}^{\square}$ f $9 \overline{)36}^{\square}$ i $8 \overline{)32}^{\square}$ l $7 \overline{)28}^{\square}$ o $7 \overline{)42}^{\square}$ r $9 \overline{)81}^{\square}$

Division with remainders

Put 17 counters into rows of 5.

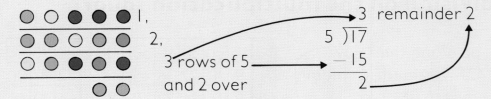

3 rows of 5 and 2 over

$$5 \overline{)17}$$
$$-15$$
$$\overline{2}$$

3 remainder 2

$17 \div 5 = 3$, remainder 2.

On a number line $17 \div 5$ is shown like this.

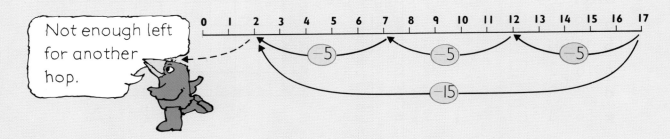

Not enough left for another hop.

$$5 \overline{)17}$$
$$-\ 5$$
$$\overline{12}$$
$$-\ 5$$
$$\overline{7}$$
$$-\ 5$$
$$\overline{2}$$

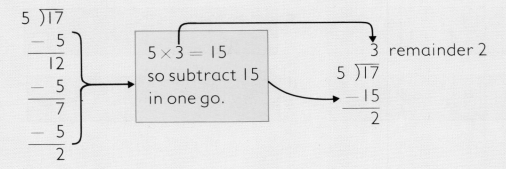

$5 \times 3 = 15$ so subtract 15 in one go.

3 remainder 2
$$5 \overline{)17}$$
$$-15$$
$$\overline{2}$$

Here are some more examples.

2 remainder 4
$$5 \overline{)14}$$
$$-10 \quad \text{(2 lots of 5)}$$
$$\overline{4}$$

3 remainder 2
$$6 \overline{)20}$$
$$-18 \quad \text{(3 lots of 6)}$$
$$\overline{2}$$

4 remainder 3
$$6 \overline{)27}$$
$$-24$$
$$\overline{3}$$

1 Copy and complete. (Use counters or a number line.)

a □ rem △
$$5 \overline{)1\ 9}$$
$$-1\ 5$$
$$\overline{4}$$

b □ rem △
$$6 \overline{)2\ 9}$$
$$-2\ 4$$
$$\overline{5}$$

c □ rem △
$$7 \overline{)3\ 8}$$
$$-3\ 5$$
$$\overline{\triangle}$$

d □ rem △
$$3 \overline{)3\ 1}$$
$$-\square$$
$$\overline{\triangle}$$

e □ rem △
$$8 \overline{)4\ 7}$$
$$-\square$$
$$\overline{\triangle}$$

1 Set these out the same way. (They all have remainders.)
Remember to leave space at the top for the answer.

a 5)22   **c** 10)37   **e** 7)45   **g** 9)75   **i** 9)89

b 6)34   **d** 9)44   **f** 3)29   **h** 4)39   **j** 8)67

Remember —
estimate,
calculate,
check.

2 Try these. (Some have remainders; some do not.)

a 2)19   **c** 5)36   **e** 8)57   **g** 10)57   **i** 9)63

b 2)18   **d** 6)36   **f** 9)64   **h** 7)50   **j** 8)64

3 **a** 34 eggs are packed into boxes, 6 in a box.
How many full boxes will there be?
How many eggs left over?

b To make a square, 4 triangles like this ▽ are fitted together ⊠
How many squares can be made from 39 triangles?
How many triangles will be left over?

c There are 7 players in a netball team.
How many teams can be formed from 32 players?
How many reserves will there be?

d You are given 60p to buy apples at 8p each.
How many can you buy and how much change will you have?

e How many pieces of ribbon 9 centimetres long can be cut
from a length 78 centimetres?
How much ribbon will be left?

f I gave 50p for 6 bags of crisps and got 2p change?
How much did each bag cost?

4 Copy and complete these "computer tapes".

÷9	10	20	30	40	50	60	70	80	90
	1 r 1								10 r 0

÷8	10	20	30	40	50	60	70	80	90
	1 r 2			5 r 0					11 r 2

Make up some more of your own. Look for patterns.

Chapter 17: Fractions

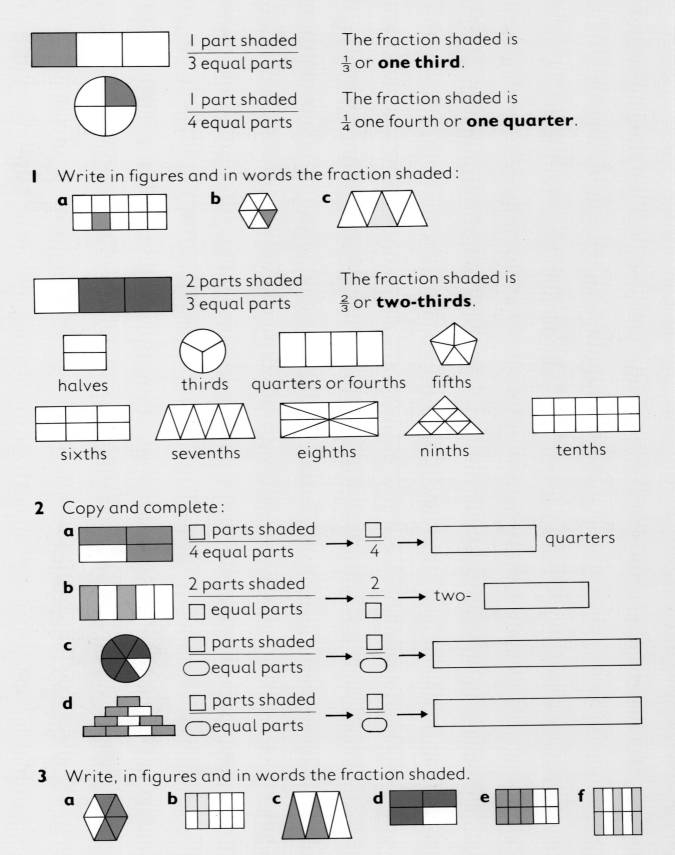

$\dfrac{\text{1 part shaded}}{\text{3 equal parts}}$ The fraction shaded is $\frac{1}{3}$ or **one third**.

$\dfrac{\text{1 part shaded}}{\text{4 equal parts}}$ The fraction shaded is $\frac{1}{4}$ one fourth or **one quarter**.

1 Write in figures and in words the fraction shaded:

a   **b**   **c**

$\dfrac{\text{2 parts shaded}}{\text{3 equal parts}}$ The fraction shaded is $\frac{2}{3}$ or **two-thirds**.

halves   thirds   quarters or fourths   fifths

sixths   sevenths   eighths   ninths   tenths

2 Copy and complete:

a $\dfrac{\square \text{ parts shaded}}{\text{4 equal parts}}$ ⟶ $\dfrac{\square}{4}$ ⟶ ☐ quarters

b $\dfrac{\text{2 parts shaded}}{\square \text{ equal parts}}$ ⟶ $\dfrac{2}{\square}$ ⟶ two- ☐

c $\dfrac{\square \text{ parts shaded}}{\bigcirc \text{equal parts}}$ ⟶ $\dfrac{\square}{\bigcirc}$ ⟶ ☐

d $\dfrac{\square \text{ parts shaded}}{\bigcirc \text{equal parts}}$ ⟶ $\dfrac{\square}{\bigcirc}$ ⟶ ☐

3 Write, in figures and in words the fraction shaded.

a   **b**   **c**   **d**   **e**   **f**

In this set of 8 circles 5 are shaded.

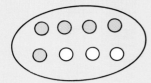 $\dfrac{5 \text{ shaded}}{8 \text{ in the whole set}} \rightarrow \dfrac{5}{8} \rightarrow$ five-eighths shaded

I Write, in figures and in words, the fraction shaded.

a 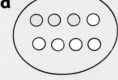 **c** 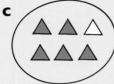 **e** 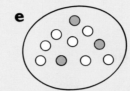 **g**

b 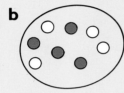 **d** 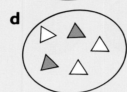 **f** 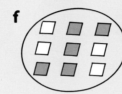 **h**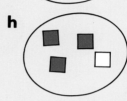

Fraction families

In each of these squares, the same fraction is shaded.

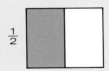 $\dfrac{1}{2}$ 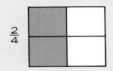 $\dfrac{2}{4}$ 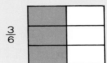 $\dfrac{3}{6}$ 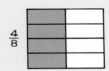 $\dfrac{4}{8}$

$\dfrac{1}{2}, \dfrac{2}{4}, \dfrac{3}{6}, \dfrac{4}{8}$ are different names for the same fraction.
They all belong to the "family of $\dfrac{1}{2}$".

2 Copy and complete: $\dfrac{1}{2} = \dfrac{2}{4} = \dfrac{3}{6} = \dfrac{4}{8} = \dfrac{5}{\square} = \dfrac{\triangle}{12} = \dfrac{10}{\square} = \dfrac{100}{\bigcirc}$

3 These diagrams show some of the "family of $\dfrac{1}{3}$".

Copy and complete:

$\dfrac{1}{3} = \dfrac{\square}{6} = \dfrac{3}{\triangle} = \dfrac{\bigcirc}{12}$

4 Write four more fractions in the "family of $\dfrac{1}{3}$".

5 Make a list of six fractions in the "family of $\dfrac{1}{5}$".

I The diagrams show $\frac{3}{4} = \frac{6}{8} = \frac{12}{16}$.

Write four more fractions in the "family of $\frac{3}{4}$".

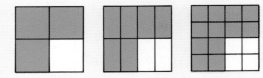

2 **a** On squared paper, draw diagrams to show that $\frac{2}{3} = \frac{4}{6} = \frac{8}{12}$
Write four more fractions in the "family of $\frac{2}{3}$".

b Do the same for $\frac{1}{5} = \frac{2}{10} = \frac{3}{15}$.

"The family of one"

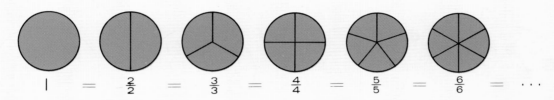

$$1 = \frac{2}{2} = \frac{3}{3} = \frac{4}{4} = \frac{5}{5} = \frac{6}{6} = \cdots$$

3 **a** Write ten more fractions in the "family of one".

b How many fractions are there in the "family of one"?

The fraction chart

4 Use strips of coloured paper or card to make a fraction chart like this.
The chart shows:
$\frac{1}{2} = \frac{2}{4} = \frac{4}{8} = \frac{3}{6} = \frac{5}{10}$

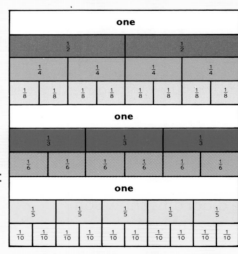

5 Use the chart to help you complete:

a $\frac{2}{3} = \frac{\square}{6}$ **c** $\frac{3}{4} = \frac{6}{\square}$ **e** $\frac{6}{10} = \frac{3}{\square}$

b $\frac{2}{5} = \frac{\square}{10}$ **d** $\frac{4}{8} = \frac{\square}{4}$ **f** $\frac{4}{\square} = \frac{8}{10}$

6 The chart also shows: $\frac{1}{2} > \frac{1}{4}$, $\frac{1}{3} < \frac{3}{8}$, $\frac{5}{6} > \frac{5}{8}$
Copy and complete by putting $>$ (more than) or $<$ (less than) between these fractions.

a $\frac{1}{2} \square \frac{1}{4}$ **c** $\frac{3}{8} \square \frac{1}{2}$ **e** $\frac{7}{8} \square \frac{2}{3}$ **g** $\frac{3}{5} \square \frac{3}{4}$ **i** $\frac{1}{2} \square \frac{1}{3} \square \frac{1}{4}$

b $\frac{1}{6} \square \frac{1}{3}$ **d** $\frac{4}{5} \square \frac{2}{3}$ **f** $\frac{1}{2} \square \frac{2}{5}$ **h** $\frac{9}{10} \square \frac{7}{8}$ **j** $\frac{3}{10} \square \frac{3}{8} \square \frac{3}{5}$

"Fraction families" from the multiplication square

The multiplication square starts at the top left hand corner with 1×1. It goes up to 10×10 in the bottom right-hand corner. Cover up most of the square but leave the top two rows showing.

1	2	3	4	5	6	7	8	9	10
2	4	6	8	10	12	14	16	18	20
3	6	9	12	15	18	21	24	27	30
4	8	12	16	20	24	28	32	36	40
5	10	15	20	25	30	35	40	45	50
6	12	18	24	30	36	42	48	54	60
7	14	21	28	35	42	49	56	63	70
8	16	24	32	40	48	56	64	72	80
9	18	27	36	45	54	63	72	81	90
10	20	30	40	50	60	70	80	90	100

1	2	3	4	5	6	7	8	9	10
2	4	6	8	10	12	14	16	18	20

From this you can list some of the members of the "family of $\frac{1}{2}$".

$\frac{1}{2} = \frac{2}{4} = \frac{3}{6} = \frac{4}{8}$ etc.

But 2 and 4 also appear in the first column of the square.

By using strips of paper we can find more members of the "family of $\frac{1}{2}$".

$\frac{2}{4} = \frac{4}{8} = \frac{6}{12} = \frac{10}{20} = \underbrace{\frac{12}{24} = \frac{14}{28} = \frac{16}{32} = \frac{18}{36} = \frac{20}{40}}_{\text{new members}}$

2	4	6	8	10	12	14	16	18	20

4	8	12	16	20	24	28	32	36	40

Even more members of the "family of $\frac{1}{2}$" can be found by going along the 3 row and the 6 row:

$\frac{3}{6} = \frac{6}{12} = \frac{9}{18} = \frac{12}{24} = \frac{15}{30} = \frac{18}{36} = \frac{21}{42}$

3	6	9	12	15	18	21	24	27	30

6	12	18	24	30	36	42	48	54	60

1 See how many more of the "family of $\frac{1}{2}$", that is fractions equal to $\frac{1}{2}$, you can find,
   a looking along the 4 row and the 8 row.
   b looking along the 5 row and the 10 row.

2 Use the multiplication square to find as many members as you can in each of these families:
   a $\frac{1}{3}$ (Use rows 1 and 3, rows 2 and 6, rows 3 and 9)
   b $\frac{3}{4}$ (rows 3 and 4, rows 6 and 8)
   c $\frac{1}{5}$ (rows 1 and 5, rows 2 and 10)
   d $\frac{2}{5}$ f $\frac{4}{5}$
   e $\frac{3}{5}$ g $\frac{2}{3}$

This line, 12cm long, is divided into 3 equal parts.

$\frac{1}{3}$ of 12cm = 4cm $\frac{2}{3}$ of 12cm = 8cm

1 Draw a line 15cm long. Divide it into 5 equal parts.

   a $\frac{1}{5}$ of 15cm is ☐cm   **b** $\frac{2}{5}$ of 15cm is ☐cm   **c** $\frac{4}{5}$ of 15cm is ☐cm

2 There are 27 children in a class and $\frac{1}{3}$ of them are boys.

   a How many boys are there in the class?
   b What fraction of the class are girls?
   c How many girls are there in the class?

3 Draw this flag and colour $\frac{1}{3}$ of the squares blue, $\frac{1}{4}$ of the squares red and leave the rest white.

   a How many squares of each colour are there?
   b What fraction of the flag is white?

4 Altogether the children in a class have 20 pets.
$\frac{1}{5}$ are cats, $\frac{2}{5}$ are dogs, $\frac{1}{10}$ are fish and $\frac{3}{10}$ rabbits.
How many of each animal are there?

Adding fractions to make 1

5 One whole divided
into 8 equal parts

1 part black
2 parts white
5 parts shaded

Fraction sentence:
$\frac{1}{8} + \frac{2}{8} + \frac{5}{8} = \frac{8}{8} = 1$

Write the fraction sentences for these:

  a   **c**   **e**   **g**   **i**

  b   **d**   **f**   **h**   **j**

Chapter 18: Time

From one time to another

Look at the two clock faces:
By counting on, you can work out
that from 9.05 to 9.27 is
22 minutes.

Start counting here

1 Copy and complete the sentences under these clocks.

a

From ☐ to ☐
is ☐ minutes.

c

From ☐ to ☐
is ☐ minutes.

b

From ☐ to ☐
is ☐ minutes.

d

From ☐ to ☐
is ☐ hours ☐ minutes.

2 a Sue should be at school by quarter past nine but she arrived at 9.32.
How many minutes late was she?

b The first half of a match started at 3.04 and lasted 45 minutes. What
time did the half-time whistle go?

c Peter put his cake into the oven at 6 minutes to 10.
When should he take it out if the baking time is 35 minutes?

d When Anne started reading, her watch showed 9:32 ; when
she finished, it said 10:45 . For how long was she reading?

Slow and fast

A clock does not always show the correct time. It may run too slowly and get behind the real time. For example, if the real time is 8.15 and the clock shows 8.10, you say, "It is 5 minutes slow" or "It has lost 5 minutes".

Some clocks go too fast and get ahead of the real time. This clock is a quarter of an hour fast.
        It has gained a quarter of an hour.

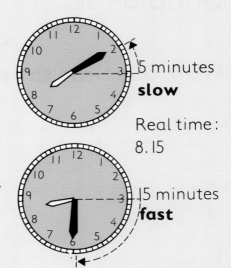

5 minutes **slow**

Real time:
8.15

15 minutes **fast**

1 If the real time is 5.49, write down how fast each of these clocks is:

a 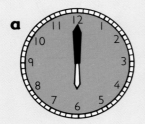   b    c    d

2 Write down how many minutes slow each of the clocks is if the real time is 7.12.

3 Write down the correct time which should be shown by each of these digital watches.

a `10:03`   b `12:38`   c `11:27`   d `10:13`

Watch **a** is 10 mins fast.

Watch **b** is 8 mins slow.

Watch **c** has lost 14 mins.

Watch **d** has gained 6 mins.

4 The clock in Gary's house gains 1 minute every day.
He puts it right at mid-day on Monday.
What time will it show at mid-day on the following Saturday?

5 The clock in Lucy's house loses half a minute a day.
How many minutes will it lose in the month of April?

6 What are two ways of finding out if your clock is showing the right time?

7 Which clock shows exactly the correct time twice every day?

a.m. and p.m.

There are 24 hours in the day.
The hour hand goes round the clock twice
in a day.

> I'll meet you at
> 8 o'clock on Saturday.

> In the morning
> or the evening?

So that you can tell the difference between 8 in the morning
and 8 in the evening, each day is split into two halves.
Times from midnight to mid-day are called **a.m.**
Times after mid-day up to the next midnight are called **p.m.**

"a.m." and "p.m." are short for Latin words –
ante meridiem ("before noon") and **post meridiem** ("after noon").

1 Find out what the words **antechamber**, **antenatal**,
postmortem, and **postscript** mean.

2 Use the diagram above like a "time ruler" to find
the number of hours between:
   a 10 a.m. on Monday and 8 p.m. on Monday
   b 4 p.m. on Monday and 1 a.m. on Tuesday
   c 11 p.m. on Sunday and noon on Monday
   d 10 p.m. on Sunday and 2 a.m. on Tuesday

3 Write these times in figures with either a.m. or p.m.
   a Twenty past eight in the morning   **d** Five minutes to midnight
   b Ten to eight in the evening   **e** One minute past noon
   c Half past two in the afternoon   **f** Twelve minutes past midnight

4 How many hours and minutes are there from 8.30 a.m. to:
   a 11.45 a.m.   **b** 1.40 p.m.   **c** 12.05 p.m.   **d** 6.20 p.m. on the same day?

The calendar

Here is a page from a calendar for
the month of October, 1981.

October 1981						
Sun	Mon	Tues	Wed	Thur	Fri	Sat
				1	2	3
4	5	6	7	8	9	10
11	12	13	14	15	16	17
18	19	20	21	22	23	24
25	26	27	28	29	30	31

1 **a** On which days of the week are
the first and last days of the month?
b How many days are there in the month?
c How many school days are there in
the month (if there are no extra holidays)?
d On which day of the week is the
2nd November?

2 Here are the months of the year in a jumbled order:
January, August, May, September, February, December, October,
March, June, April, July, November.

a Write them down in the right order.
b Four of these months have 30 days in them.
Write their names down.
c Which month usually has 28 days?
How many does it sometimes have? When does this happen?

3 Ann's 9th birthday is on 30th September 1981.
Mary's 9th birthday is on 3rd November 1981.
Who is older, and by how many days?

4 Mary writes the date when she was born like this: 3.11.72.

a What does the 3 stand for? What does the 11 stand for?
What is the 72 short for?
b Can you write this date in two other ways?
c How old will she be on her birthday in 1987?

5 Write the dates when these events happen.

a Christmas Day   **c** St. Valentine's Day   **e** April Fool's Day
b New Year's Day   **d** St. Swithen's Day   **f** Chrismas Eve

1 Look at the fourth column of the calendar (under Wed.).
   a Where have you seen these numbers before?
   b Why do they happen here?

2 How many days are there in: **a** 3 weeks?   **b** 5 weeks?

3 How many weeks are there in: **a** 63 days?   **b** 42 days?

4 Here is a page from a calendar, but the bottom has been torn off.

JANUARY 1982						
Sun	Mon	Tues	Wed	Thur	Fri	Sat
					1	2

   a Draw the full calendar page for January in your book and fill in all the missing days.
   b What day of the week will the 51st day of the year be?
   c What day of the week will 17th February fall on?
   d What day of the week will 1st March fall on?

Leap years

Look at these pages from calendars for 1983 and 1984.

There is an extra day in 1984 because 1984 is a **leap year**.

A leap year has 366 days instead of 365.

The extra day is given to February because it is the shortest month.

FEBRUARY 1983						
S	M	T	W	T	F	S
		1	2	3	4	5
6	7	8	9	10	11	12
13	14	15	16	17	18	19
20	21	22	23	24	25	26
27	28					

FEBRUARY 1984						
S	M	T	W	T	F	S
		1	2	3	4
5	6	7	8	9	10	11
12	13	14	15	16	17	18
19	20	21	22	23	24	25
26	27	28	29			

5 Here are some more leap years: 1960, 1964, 1968, 1972, 1976, 1980.
   a What is the pattern for leap years?
   b Write a list of the next 5 leap years beginning with 1984.
   c Find out why we have leap years.
   d Do you know anyone whose birthday is on February 29th? What do they do about their birthdays on non-leap years?

Chapter 19: Multiplication 2

Multiplying in parts

The soldier has
14 buttons on his coat.
7 in each column:

$7 \times 2 = 14$

Now he has his belt on.

Above the belt: $4 \times 2 = 8$

Below the belt: $3 \times 2 = \underline{6}$

Altogether: $\underline{14}$

Instead of multiplying 7×2:

Separate into parts: $(4+3) \times 2$

Multiply each part on its own:

Add the parts together again.

$4 \times 2 = 8$

$3 \times 2 = 6$

$\left.\begin{array}{c} \\ \\ \end{array}\right\}$ 14

This time 8×4 is separated into parts.

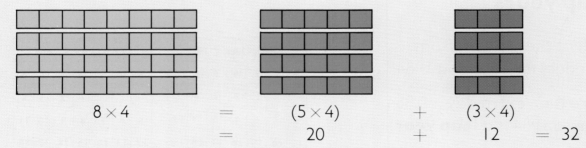

$$8 \times 4 \qquad = \qquad (5 \times 4) \qquad + \qquad (3 \times 4)$$
$$= \qquad 20 \qquad + \qquad 12 \qquad = 32$$

1 Use cubes or counters for these.

a $5 \times 4 = (3 \times 4) + (2 \times 4)$
$= 12 + \bigcirc = \square$

e $9 \times 5 = (5 \times 5) + (\square \times 5)$
$= 25 + \bigcirc = \square$

b $9 \times 4 = (6 \times 4) + (3 \times 4)$
$= \bigcirc + 12 = \square$

f $8 \times 7 = (6 \times 7) + (\square \times 7)$
$= 42 + \bigcirc = \square$

c $9 \times 4 = (7 \times 4) + (2 \times 4)$
$= \bigcirc + 8 = \square$

g $8 \times 7 = (\square \times 7) + (3 \times 7)$
$= \bigcirc + 21 = \square$

d $9 \times 5 = (6 \times 5) + (3 \times 5)$
$= \bigcirc + 15 = \square$

h $7 \times 6 = (4 \times 6) + (\square \times 6)$
$= 24 + \bigcirc = \square$

Multiplying tens and unit by units

Splitting a number into parts and multiplying each part
separately is useful for larger numbers.

The diagram shows 13 × 4

13 × 4 is set out like this:

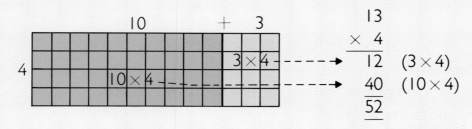

$$
\begin{array}{r}
13 \\
\times\ 4 \\
\hline
12 \quad (3 \times 4) \\
40 \quad (10 \times 4) \\
\hline
52 \\
\hline
\end{array}
$$

I Set out the multiplications in the same way for these:

a 12 × 4

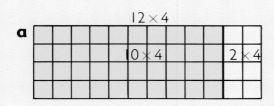

d 15 × 5

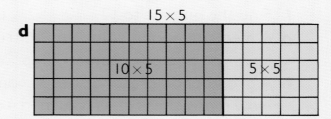

b 11 × 6

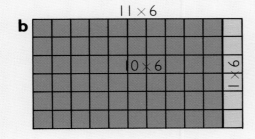

e 16 × 3

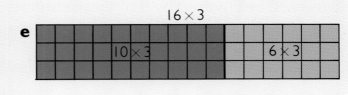

c 14 × 5

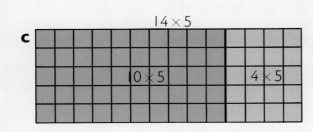

f 13 × 7

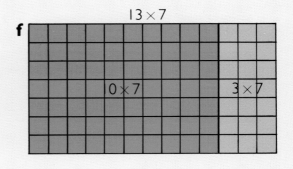

This diagram shows 24 × 3:

It is set out like this:

$$
\begin{array}{r}
24 \\
\times\ 3 \\
\hline
12 \quad (4 \times 3) \\
60 \quad (20 \times 3) \\
\hline
72 \\
\hline
\end{array}
$$

1 Remember — estimate, calculate, check.
Set these out the same way:

a 13 × 5	**e** 14 × 7	**i** 22 × 8	**m** 31 × 6
b 17 × 3	**f** 13 × 9	**j** 29 × 5	**n** 37 × 3
c 19 × 2	**g** 21 × 4	**k** 27 × 6	**o** 42 × 4
d 16 × 7	**h** 26 × 3	**l** 23 × 7	**p** 53 × 5

2 **a** How many eggs are there altogether in 17 boxes with 6 eggs in each box?

b Seats for a concert are set out in 8 rows with 14 in a row. How many seats are there?

c What is the product of 13 and 9?

d How much will it cost to take 7 children for a bus ride if the fare is 16 pence each?

e If a crayon weighs 26 grams, what do 4 crayons weigh?

f Find the answer to 12 + 12 + 12 + 12 + 12 + 12 by multiplication.

g A medicine spoon holds 5 millilitres. How much medicine have you had after taking 27 spoonfuls?

h A gramophone record does 33 complete turns every minute. How many times does it turn in 4 minutes?

i The area of a stamp is 13 square centimetres. What area will be covered by 8 of these stamps?

j A racing car travels 38 metres in a second. How far does it go in 6 seconds?

3 Copy and complete, then look for patterns:

factor	16	32	64	14	28	21	42	12	36	18	12
factor	8	4	2	6	3	4	2	7	2	4	6
product											

4

21	14	19
16	18	20
17	22	15

Multiply each number in this magic square by 2. Check that your new square is "magic" by adding rows, columns and diagonals.
Make up some more magic squares by multiplying by 3, 4, 5 etc.

Chapter 20: Money 2

More writing in pounds and pence

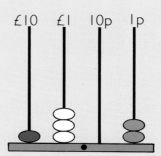

The abacus records £13 and 2 pence.
You write £13·02.
You must show that one of
the abacus columns is empty
by putting a zero in that place.
Remember the zero tells you there were no ten pence.

1 Draw an abacus to record each of the following amounts.
   a £34·06   **b** £5·04   **c** £30·60   **d** £38·05   **e** £20·90   **f** £34·02

Because there are one hundred pence in one pound.
you can write either £1·00 or 100p.
One pound and thirty-five pence can be written as £1·35 or 135p.

2 Write these amounts in two ways.
   First write them in pounds then in pence.
   a Five pounds and forty-nine pence
   b Fifteen pounds and sixty-eight pence
   c Sixteen pounds and twenty-three pence

3 Write these amounts in pounds: **a** 456p   **b** 372p   **c** 914p   **d** 802p

4 Write these amounts in pence: **a** £5·71   **b** £3·66   **c** £9·92   **d** £7·08

Listing amounts of money

5 Write these amounts in pounds.
   Put them in columns, keeping the decimal points under each other,
   like this:

	£
£1·23, 46p, £4·00, £0·06	1·23
	0·46
	4·00
	0·06

   a £2·35, 27p, £5, 6p
   b £2·04, 81p, £10, 1p
   c 1p, £4·50, 75p, 190p
   d £1, 1p, 234p, £6·32

I Write these amounts in pence.
Put them in columns like this:

87p, 8p, £1·34, 105p

p
87
8
134
105

a 56p, £2·16, 63p, 5p
b 103p, £1·63, 53p, 5p
c £2, 99p, 14p, 9p
d 10p, 20p, £2·56, 2p

2 In a gift shop these items are on sale.

 book £1·05   teddybear £3·99    tennis racket £4   crayons 85p

 camera £4·50    draughts £1·25   pencil case 50p

a Write a list of the gifts which have prices less than £1.
b Write a list of the gifts which cost more than £1 but less than £2.
c List the gifts which cost more than £2.
d Write a list of the gifts with their prices in order, starting from the cheapest.
e If 10p is taken off each of the prices, make a list of the gifts showing their new prices.
f If 20p is added to each of the prices shown in the picture make a list of the gifts with their new prices.

Other ways of saying prices

Bargain price £1·68

When we go shopping we sometimes call this amount "one pound, sixty-eight" or "one sixty-eight".

We mean one pound and sixty-eight pence, which is written as £1·68.

3 Here are some for you to do. Record these amounts in figures.
a One pound forty-five
b Three pounds sixty-one
c Five ninety-nine
d Two pounds four pence
e Twelve fifty
f One pound ten pence
g Ten pounds
h Seven pounds seventy
i One penny less than £3

Addition of money

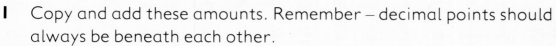

Estimate first by rounding to the nearest £ (midway mark 50p).

1 Copy and add these amounts. Remember – decimal points should always be beneath each other.

a £	**b** £	**c** £	**d** £	**e** £	**f** £
3·32	3·36	5·05	5·19	7·41	6·89
+1·53	+2·12	+2·12	+2·34	+3·48	+2·34
4·14	3·41	1·47	3·57	2·65	1·35

g £5·83+£2·50+£2·33   **h** £3·32+£4·93+£4·47

2 a I spent £1·05 on a book, £4·75 on a record and 75p on a packet of crayons. How much did I spend altogether?

 b Jill has £5 for her birthday. She would like to buy a scrap book for £1·25, a pair of scissors for £2·56 and some new paints for £1·05. Can she afford to buy them all?

Finding the change by counting on

3 Find the change by counting on in these examples. Use your coins if you need them. Copy and complete the table.

	price	amount given to shopkeeper	change
a	65p	£1·00	
b	£0·42	£1·00	
c	£1·24	£2·00	
d	£1·51	£2·00	

	price	amount given to shopkeeper	change
e	£2·21	£3·00	
f	£0·19	£1·00	
g	£3·64	£4·00	
h	£1·55	£2·00	

Subtraction of money

Estimate first by rounding to the nearest £.

I Copy and complete the following subtractions. Remember – the decimal points should always be beneath one another.

	a £	**b** £	**c** £	**d** £	**e** £	**f** £
	8·76	7·43	5·37	6·17	7·60	8·00
	−2·54	−2·27	−3·48	−3·38	−2·49	−4·32

Multiplication of money

The cost of 4kg of potatoes at 15p per kg can be found by addition, but multiplying is quicker.
4kg will cost:

15p + 15p + 15p + 15p

```
  15p
×  4
───
  20   (5 × 4)
  40   (10 × 4)
───
  60p
```

Complete these:

2 a 6kg of potatoes at 14p per kg   **e** 5 metres of wire at 18p per metre
 b 7 metres of cord at 13p per metre   **f** 4kg of cheese at 50p per ½kg
 c 4 litres of beer at 24p per litre   **g** Half a dozen eggs at 8p each
 d 2kg of sweets at 23p per 500g   **h** 8m² carpet at £12 per m²

Division of money

3 a 4 eggs cost 28p. What is the cost of 1 egg?
 b How many children can be given 5p each from 45p?
 c Share 63p equally between 7 children.
 d If 8 metres of ribbon cost 56p, find the cost of one metre.
 e How many pence in $\frac{1}{5}$ of a pound?

Chapter 21: Volume and Capacity 2

Using capacity measures

If you want to put 75ml of water into a jar, here are two ways to measure the right amount.

The first way is to fill the 50ml, 20ml and 5ml containers and empty them all into the jar.

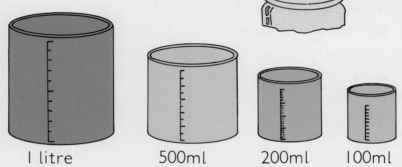

The other way is to use a measure bigger than 75ml with a scale of ml marked down the side.

These measures come in different sizes.

1 litre   500ml   200ml   100ml

To measure 75ml you take the 100ml measure and fill it till the water reaches the 75ml mark.

Do you know why the 100ml measure has been used and not one of the bigger ones?

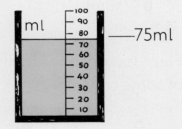

1   Use the first way (with smaller measures) to measure out the following amounts of water. Record in your book the containers you have used each time.

a 25ml	**c** 85ml	**e** 140ml	**g** 350ml	**i** 885ml
b 60ml	**d** 110ml	**f** 165ml	**h** 720ml	**j** 915ml

2   Use the second way (with a marked measure) to measure out the following amounts of water. Record in your book the smallest container which will hold each amount.

a 35ml	**c** 95ml	**e** 250ml	**g** 490ml	**i** 750ml
b 60ml	**d** 120ml	**f** 350ml	**h** 625ml	**j** 1000ml

Millilitres as fractions of a litre

Look at this set
of measures.
There is a new one –
250ml.

1 litre 500ml 250ml 200ml 100ml 50ml

1 a How many times can the 250ml container be filled from
   the 1 litre container? (Try to work this out without
   using real containers.)
   b What fraction is 250ml of 1 litre?
   c Which container holds $\frac{1}{2}$ litre?
   d If the 200ml container is filled twice from the $\frac{1}{2}$ litre container, how
   many ml of water would be left in the larger container?
   e How many times must the 50ml container be filled to make $\frac{1}{4}$ litre?
   f How many ml are there in $\frac{3}{4}$ litre?

2 Copy and complete
   a $\frac{1}{2}$ litre $+ \square$ ml $= 1$ litre   **c** $\square$ ml $+ 250$ ml $= \frac{3}{4}$ litre
   b 750 ml $+ \square$ ml $= 1$ litre   **d** 150 ml $+ \square$ ml $= \frac{1}{4}$ litre

Here is a graph showing the capacities
of some containers.

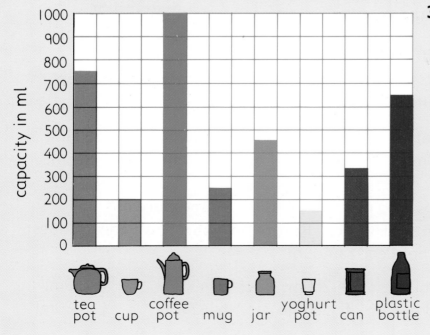

3 Look at the graph
   carefully and answer
   these questions.
   a How much does
   the cup hold?
   b What is the capacity
   of the jar?
   c Which holds $\frac{3}{4}$
   litre?
   d Could you fill 2
   cups from the can?
   e How many more
   millilitres does a mug
   hold than a cup?

The marks on I litre measures

These I litre measures have sides marked in ml.
(Remember, there are 1000ml in I litre.)
They contain different amounts of water.

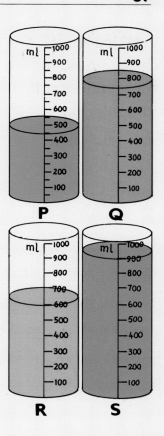

P **Q**

R **S**

I **a** How many ml of water are there in measure **P**?
  b How many ml of water are there in measure **Q**?
  c How many more ml are needed to fill measure **Q**?
  d Which of the two measures together have enough
     water in them to make 1½ litres?
  e By how many ml is the water in **R** less than I litre?
  f How many 150ml glasses can be filled from **S**?
  g How much more water is shown in **S** than in **R**?

More than a litre

In this bottle is I litre and 650 millilitres of fruit juice.
To record this you could write: I litre and 650ml.
Another way is to write litres
and millilitres in separate columns.
An even shorter way is to separate litres and
millilitres with a **decimal point**.

	litres	ml	
I litre and 650ml	I	650	1·650 litres

2 Copy and complete this table.

		litres	ml	litres
a	2 litres and 450ml	2	450	2·450
b	3 litres and 250ml	☐	☐	☐
c	5 litres and 180ml	☐	☐	☐
d	☐ litres ☐ml	☐	☐	4·550
e	☐ litres and ☐ml	☐	☐	3·820

Look carefully at the liquid in these measuring jars:

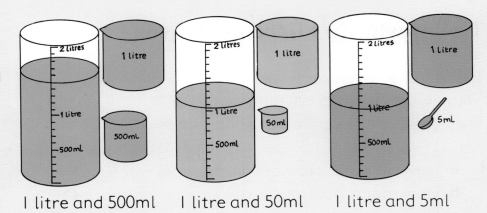

I litre and 500ml   I litre and 50ml   I litre and 5ml

How do we write down these capacities?

	litres	ml		
I litre and 500ml	I	5 0 0	1·500 litres
I litre and 50ml	I	5 0	1·050 litres
I litre and 5ml	I	5	1·005 litres

1·050 litres — This shows that there are **no** hundreds of millilitres. The number of millilitres is **less than 100**.

1·005 litres — These show that there are **no** hundreds and **no** tens of millilitres. The number of millilitres is **less than 10**.

1 Copy and complete.

a 2 litres and 700ml
b 2 litres and 70ml
c 2 litres and   7ml
d 3 litres and 255ml
e I litre and 75ml
f 950ml
g 95ml

litres	ml			
2	700	=	2·700	litres
☐	☐	=	☐	litres
☐	☐	=	☐	litres
☐	☐	=	☐	litres
☐	☐	=	☐	litres
☐	☐	=	☐	litres
☐	☐	=	☐	litres

2 Use the I litre measure and any smaller measures you need to find the capacity of some larger containers. Estimate the capacity first; pour I litre of water if it helps you to estimate.

Record like this:

container	estimate litres	measurement litres
bucket	8·500	9·730

Chapter 22: Division 2

Division – larger numbers

For 91 ÷ 7, we could put out 91 counters in rows of 7
and count the rows. This would take a long time.

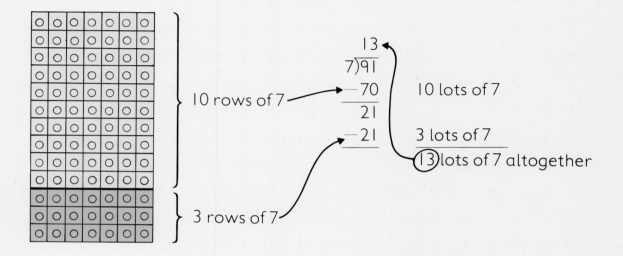

Because 7 × 10 = 70 and 70 < 91 we take away 10 lots of 7 first.
This leaves a smaller number to split into lots of 7.

1 Here are some more diagrams. Look carefully at each one
then copy and complete the written part.

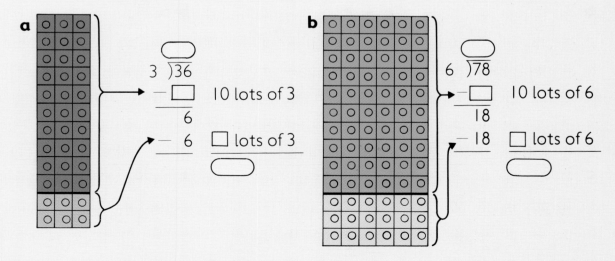

I Copy and complete

Remember – estimate, calculate, check.

a 4)6 4
◯
  − ☐ | I 0 lots of 4
  2 4
  − 2 4 | ☐ lots of 4
        ◯ lots of 4

c 5)8 5
◯
  − ☐ | I 0 lots of 5
  3 5
  − 3 5 | ☐ lots of 5
        ◯ lots of 5

e 6)9 6
◯
  − ☐ | I 0 lots of 6
  3 6
  − 3 6 | ☐ lots of 6
        ◯ lots of 6

b 8)9 6
◯
  − ☐ | I 0 lots of 8
  I 6
  − I 6 | ☐ lots of 8
        ◯ lots of 8

d 7)9 8
◯
  − ☐ | I 0 lots of 7
  2 8
  − ☐ | ☐ lots of 7
        ◯ lots of 7

f 4)7 6
◯
  − ☐ | I 0 lots of 4
  3 6
  − ☐ | ☐ lots of 4
        ◯ lots of 4

2 a 2)3 2
I 0 + ☐ = ◯
  − ☐ | I 0 (2)
  I 2
  − ☐ | ☐ (2)

d 3)5 7
I 0 + ☐ = ◯
  − ☐ | I 0 (3)
  2 7
  − ☐ | ☐ (3)

g 6)8 4
I 0 + ☐ = ◯
  − ☐ | I 0 (6)
  2 4
  − ☐ | ☐ (6)

b 3)4 5
I 0 + ☐ = ◯
  − ☐ | I 0 (3)
  I 5
  − ☐ | ☐ (3)

e 4)6 8
I 0 + ☐ = ◯
  − ☐ | I 0 (4)
  2 8
  − ☐ | ☐ (4)

h 6)9 0
I 0 + ☐ = ◯
  − ☐ | I 0 (6)
  3 0
  − ☐ | ☐ (6)

c 3)5 I
I 0 + ☐ = ◯
  − ☐ | I 0 (3)
  2 I
  − ☐ | ☐ (3)

f 5)8 0
I 0 + ☐ = ◯
  − ☐ | I 0 (5)
  3 0
  − ☐ | ☐ (5)

i 7)8 4
I 0 + ☐ = ◯
  − ☐ | I 0 (7)
  I 4
  − ☐ | 2 (7)

Division with remainders

Remember — estimate, calculate, check.

1 Copy and complete

                 1 0 + 7 = 17   1 0 + 4 = 14   1 0 + ☐ = ◯

a   2)3 5   **b**   3)4 4   **c**   4)6 3

        − ☐   − ☐   − 4 0

         1 5   1 4   2 3

        − 1 4   − 1 2   − ☐

             1 remainder   △ remainder   △ remainder

2 Set these out in the same way:

a 2)33   **c** 3)29   **e** 7)97   **g** 8)98   **i** 6)94

b 3)41   **d** 4)65   **f** 6)83   **h** 5)89   **j** 9)100

3 a To make a hexagon ⬡ six triangles like this △ are fitted together.
How many hexagons can be made from 89 triangles?
How many triangles are left?

b 75 pencils are put into boxes with 4 in each box.
How many full boxes will there be and how many pencils left over?

c How many days are there altogether in March, April and May?
How many full weeks is this?

d A medicine spoon holds 5 millilitres.
How many spoonfuls can you pour from a bottle holding
88 millilitres and how much is left in the bottle?

e How many books 4 centimetres wide can be placed side by side
on a shelf 50 centimetres long?

f In the dining hall, 6 children sit at each table.
If there are 89 children how many full tables
will there be?

g How many teams of 7 can be formed from 90 children?
How many will not be in a team?

Chapter 23: Weight 2

Scales with a dial

Many kinds of scales do not need weights.
A pointer points to a mark on a dial
to show the weight.
The letter weighs 100g.
These kitchen scales show that
the apples weigh 300g.

1 Record the weights shown on this dial
When the pointer is at **A**, **B**, **C** and **D**.

If the pointer stops between two figures you have
to work out what the marks stand for.

Pointer **E** is halfway between 200 and 300,
that is 250 grams.

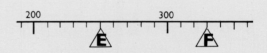

Each little mark stands for 10g.
Count on in 10's from 300 up to pointer **F**, that is 330 grams.

2 Copy and complete.
  a The weights on
   the dial are
   numbered every☐g.
  b The pointer marked
   letter☐ is midway
   between 0 and 200g.
  c The small markings
   stand for ☐ g each.

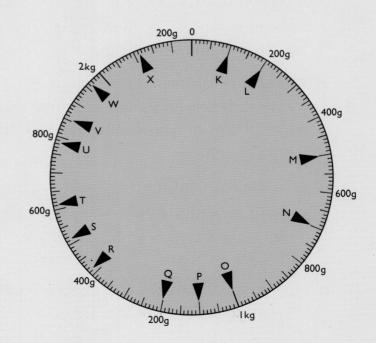

3 Record the weights shown
   by all the letters K to X.

Grams and kilograms

An object weighs 1kg and 350g. You can write 1kg and 350g.
A better way is to write kg and g in separate columns.
An even shorter way is to separate the kg and the g with a
decimal point.

	kg	g	
1kg and 350g	1	350	1·350kg

1 Copy and complete this table.

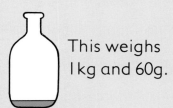

kg | g

a 3kg and 250g = ☐ ☐ = ☐

b 1kg and 900g = ☐ ☐ = ☐

c 6kg and 630g = ☐ ☐ = ☐

d 10·700kg = ☐ ☐ = ☐

e 0·325kg = ☐ ☐ = ☐

This weighs
1kg and 600g.

This weighs
1kg and 60g.

This empty
bottle weighs
1kg and 6g.

1·060 kg
ᒣ—This shows that
there are NO hundreds
of grams. The number
of grams is *less than 100*.

1·006 kg
ᒣᒣ—These show
that there are NO
hundreds and NO
tens of grams.
The number of
grams is *less than 10*.

kg | g

1kg and 600g = 1 | 600 = 1·600kg
1kg and 60g = 1 | 60 = 1·060kg
1kg and   6g = 1 | 6 = 1·006kg

kg | g

2 a 3kg and 80g = ☐ ☐ = ☐ kg
  b 3kg and   8g = ☐ ☐ = ☐ kg
  c 1kg and 90g = ☐ ☐ = ☐ kg

Weights on packets

Most food packets are marked with their weight in grams.
We always write grams or g for short.

1 Copy this list out on a piece of paper.
Take the list home. Find as many of
the items as you can.
Write down the weight it says
on each packet.

Collect empty packets and labels from
cans, and lists of things which show
weights in kilograms or grams.

food packet	weight in g
packet of tea	
packet of soup	
can of fruit	
salad cream	
bottle of sauce	
packet of jelly	
can of meat	
packet of cereal	

Parts of a kilogram

2 Some kinds of cheese are sold
in long blocks. Here are three
1 kg slices taken from a block.

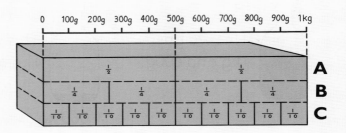

3 Copy and complete: (The picture will help you.)

  a Slice **A** is cut into two $\frac{1}{2}$ pieces. Each piece weighs ☐ g.

  b Slice **B** is cut into four $\frac{1}{4}$ pieces. Each piece weighs ☐ g.

  c Slice **C** is cut into ten $\frac{1}{10}$ pieces. Each piece weighs ☐ g.

  d $\frac{1}{4}$ kg = ☐ g   **e** $\frac{3}{4}$ kg = ☐ g   **f** $\frac{3}{10}$ kg = ☐ g   **g** $\frac{7}{10}$ kg = ☐ g

Very heavy things

When weighing very heavy things
we use kilograms only.

4 List 10 other objects or animals
heavier than 1 kg and estimate how heavy they are.

5 Make a list of the weights of four children in your class.

Chapter 24: Negative numbers

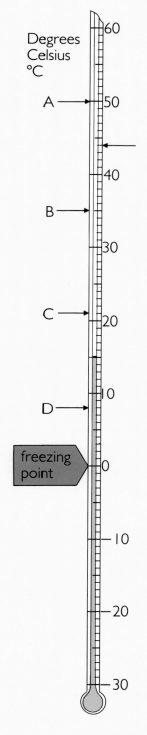

Thermometers measure temperature. This is a Celsius thermometer with a scale of 100 units or **degrees** between zero, the freezing point of water, and one hundred, the boiling point of water.

This reading is 44°C (44 degrees Celsius)

1 What reading does the thermometer show?

2 What are the readings at A, B, C and D?

3 What is the normal body temperature in degrees Celsius?

4 Draw a horizontal thermometer scale like this on squared paper.

Mark on your scale these readings recorded in July:

Innsbruck 24°C; Stockholm 19°C; York 13°C

In winter, when it is very cold, the temperature can drop below freezing point. In January these temperatures were recorded:

Innsbruck ‾27°C; Stockholm ‾24°C; York ‾14°C

Find these readings on the thermometer picture. Notice that a reading **below zero** is written with a raised minus sign and is read as **minus** (or **negative**) **degrees Celsius**

The zero mark separates all the negative readings on one side from all the positive readings on the other side:

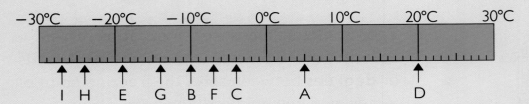

1 On squared paper draw a Celsius scale like this one and write down what the readings are at A, B, C, D, E, F, G, H and I.

2 Which letters show the January readings for Innsbruck, Stockholm and York?

Negative numbers on the calculator

On your calculator press these keys in turn:

The result shows as a negative number, $^-2$
The calculator shows what happens on number line with both negative and positive numbers: Start at 3, hop back 5, land on $^-2$

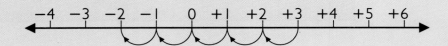

3 Try these on your calculator and record the results:
  a $5-7=\boxed{}$ **e** $2-11=\boxed{}$
  b $6-9=\boxed{}$ **f** $11-15=\boxed{}$
  c $11-16=\boxed{}$ **g** $30-40=\boxed{}$
  d $8-10=\boxed{}$ **h** $0-7=\boxed{}$

4 Think of some more keys you can press to give a negative result in the display. Write them down.

5 Which key must you press first for these?

  a $\boxed{}-3=^-2$ **e** $\boxed{}-6=^-3$
  b $\boxed{}-4=^-1$ **f** $\boxed{}-11=^-1$
  c $\boxed{}-12=^-5$ **g** $\boxed{}-15=^-5$
  d $\boxed{}-6=^-6$ **h** $\boxed{}-21=^-14$

The two way race

For this game you will need:
Two dice: one normal, numbered 1 to 6,
one with 2 green faces, 2 red, 1 yellow and 1 white;
a different coloured cube, counter or token for each player;
a number line from − 15 to + 15 with 0 in the middle.

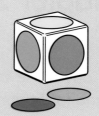

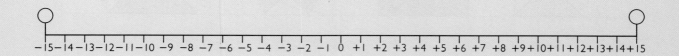

Each player starts with his or her token on zero.
Then each player in turn rolls both dice; one for the direction,
one for the distance. For example:
green and **3** means go forward **3** steps,

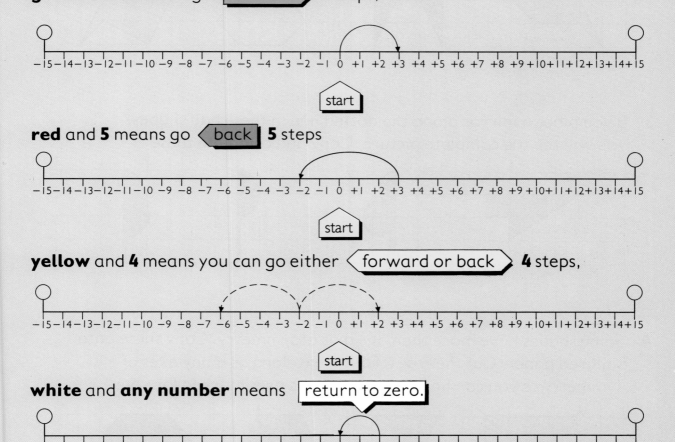

red and **5** means go back **5** steps

yellow and **4** means you can go either forward or back **4** steps,

white and **any number** means return to zero.

The winner is the first player to pass − 15 or + 15 at **either end** of the
number line.

Chapter 25: Shape 2

1 Copy these shapes onto squared paper. Cut them out
and fold them so that one part fits exactly on the other.
The fold is an **axis of symmetry**.

2 Copy these shapes onto squared paper and draw in
their axes of symmetry.

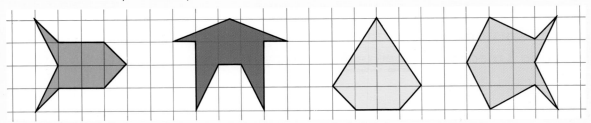

3 If you place a mirror along the dotted line in these half shapes
you will see the complete picture. Copy and complete these:

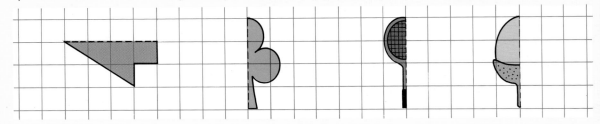

4 Some shapes have more than one axis of symmetry. Copy these onto
squared paper. Cut them out. Fold them along as many axes of
symmetry as you can find. The first has its axes marked for you.

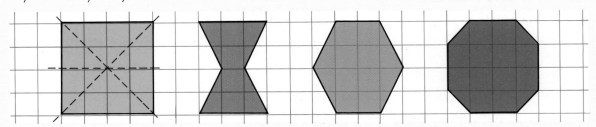

1 Some of the capital letters of the alphabet have axes of symmetry.
Make a list of them marking the axes of symmetry.
Here are the first three.

2 Cut out a large square from a piece of paper.
Fold it into two equal parts along the axis
of symmetry shown in the diagram.
(How do you know the two parts are equal?)

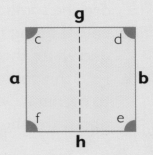

> Every time we fold a shape along an axis of symmetry we discover
> something about the shape because sides and angles which fit on
> each other are equal.

The fold shows that side **a** is the same length as side **b** and that
angle **c** is the same size as angle **d**. What other two angles are equal?

3 Unfold the cut-out shape and then fold it
along the axis of symmetry shown in this diagram.
Copy and complete the following sentences.

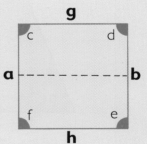

  a Side **g** is the same length as side ☐.
  b Angle **c** is the same size as angle ☐.
  c Angle **e** is the same size as angle ☐.

4 Unfold the cut-out square and then fold it along
the axis of symmetry shown in this diagram.
Copy and complete the following.

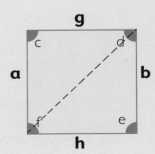

  a Side **a** is the same length as side ☐.
  b Side **g** is the same length as side ☐.
  c Angle **c** is the same size as angle ☐.

1 Cut a large oblong from a piece of paper and letter the sides and angles as in the diagram.

a Fold it along the horizontal axis of symmetry.

b Write a sentence about sides which are equal.

c Write two sentences about angles which are the same size.

d Fold it along the vertical line of symmetry and write three similar sentences.

e Fold the oblong along a diagonal (corner to corner). Does this tell you anything about the shape?

2 Copy this triangle onto a piece of squared paper and cut it out.

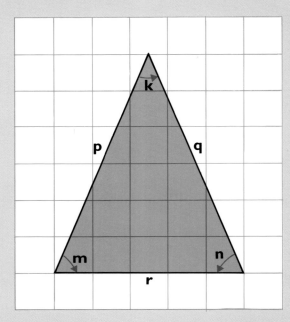

a Fold it along its axis of symmetry.

b Fold and complete one of the following:

Side **p** is the same length as side ☐

Angle **m** is the same size as angle ☐

This triangle has a special name.

It is called an **isosceles triangle**.

The word isosceles comes from two Greek words which mean equal legs.

We can see why from this drawing.

1 This shape is called an **equilateral triangle**.
Trace it onto a piece of paper and cut it out.

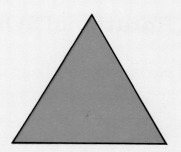

a How many axes of symmetry are there?
b What can you discover about its sides?
c Write a sentence about the angles.

2 Copy these shapes onto squared paper.

Cut them out.

On each one write how many axes of symmetry you can discover
then mark with the same colour the sides which are equal.

Do the same for angles which are the same size.

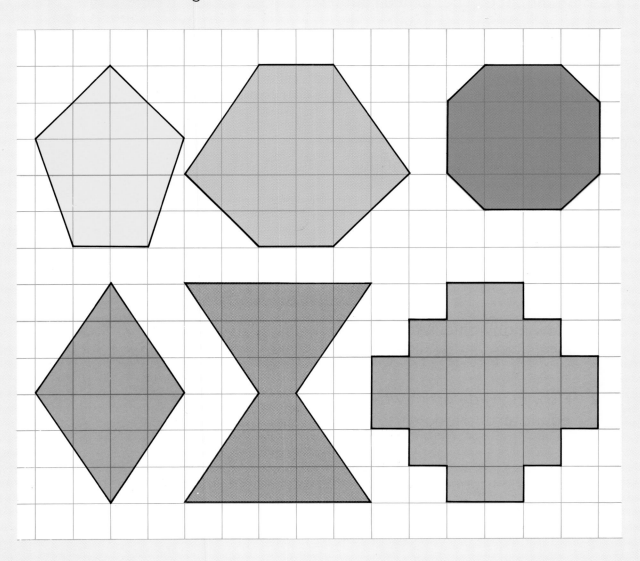

Rotational Symmetry

Have you ever tried fitting a jigsaw together upside down?
(The jigsaw upside down — not you!)
There is no picture to help you, only the shape of the piece and the hole which it fits.
Whichever way you turn it, each piece fits in only one way.

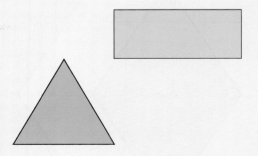

This is not like a set of mosaic shapes.
Some shapes can be turned round to fit in more than one way.

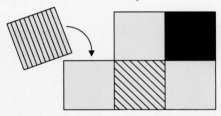

The square will fit into the corner. You can turn the square round and it still fits.

A square will fit into its outline 4 different ways.

1 How many different ways will an oblong fit into its outline?

2 How many different ways will an equilateral triangle fit?

Because the square, oblong and equilateral triangle fit into their own outlines in more than one way, they have **rotational symmetry.**

3 Draw some more shapes you think have rotational symmetry.

Testing for rotational symmetry

Draw a square with 3 cm sides.
(Use a template if you have one.)
Copy its outline on tracing paper.
Now you have two identical squares.

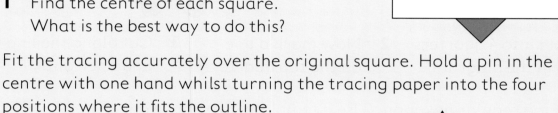

I Find the centre of each square.
What is the best way to do this?

Fit the tracing accurately over the original square. Hold a pin in the centre with one hand whilst turning the tracing paper into the four positions where it fits the outline.

2 Test the equilateral triangle in the same way. The lines on the diagram show you how to find the centre of the triangle.

3 Test your own shapes and try these. Trace them and rotate to find how many times each will fit into its outline.

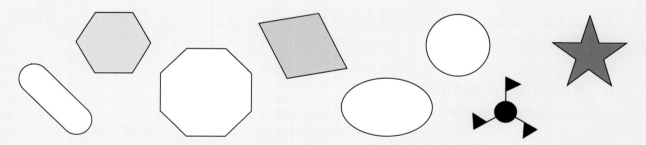

4 There are many designs and trademarks which have rotational symmetry. Make a collection of some.

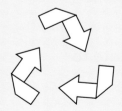
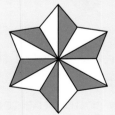
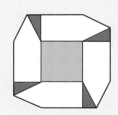

The pattern of a crossword is usually symmetrical. Some will rotate and fit in 4 ways, others in only 2 ways. Add some examples from newspapers and magazines to your collection.

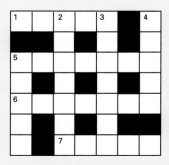

Rotational patterns

a Paper folding

Cut out a square with sides of 10 centimetres.

1 Fold into 4 quarters as in the diagram

2 Now mark a line on the top quarter.

3 Cut along the line and open out

Cut out a regular hexagon. (Use a template if you have one.)

1 Fold along the diagonals.

2 Mark out a shape on the top triangle.

3 Cut out the shape and open out.

Try some patterns of your own and test them to see how many times each one fits into its outline.

b Rotating a template

Fold a square backing sheet into 4 quarters, either along the diagonals or the medians. Cut out a template from a piece of card.

Use a pin or paper fastener to fix near the edge of the template to the centre of the square backing sheet.
Line up with one of the folds and draw round the template.
Rotate the template to the next fold and repeat.

Chapter 26: Probability

Is it fair?

A game for two players.

You will need a die marked with

3 circles ◯◯◯ , I square ☐ , I triangle △ , I oblong ▭

The red player has 6 red counters
and a red bingo card.

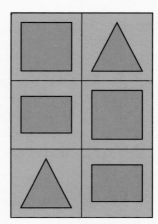

The blue player has 6 blue counters
and a blue bingo card.

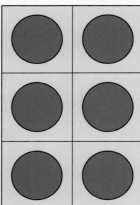

Take turns to roll the die.
Each time a shape on your bingo card
comes up, cover it with your coloured counter.

The first player to fill his or her card is the winner.

1 Which bingo card is likely to be the winner?

2 Is the game fair? Give your reasons.

3 Play the game 10 times.
Did each player win about the same number of times?
Do you think the game is fair or unfair? Give your reasons.

The truth game

Anna, Gary and Jane each rolled a fair die 300 times.
They recorded how many times they scored each number
on a **frequency chart**.

Only one of them was telling the truth. The other two were lying.

frequency (number of times)			
score	Anna	Gary	Jane
⚀	35	50	47
⚁	36	50	52
⚂	43	50	46
⚃	32	50	58
⚄	120	50	46
⚅	34	50	51

1 a Who was telling the truth?
  b Why do you think the other two were lying?

2 Copy and complete these statements, choosing words from this list:

**very likely; very unlikely; almost certain; almost impossible;
Anna; Gary; Jane;**

a It is .... that .... was telling the truth.

b It is .... that .... was telling the truth.

c It is .... that .... was telling a lie.

d It is .... that Anna threw a ⚄
120 times out of 300 throws.

e I think it would be .... to get a result like Gary's.

Rolling two dice

This table shows all the possible totals you can get by adding the spots scored on two dice.

For example, if and are rolled, 8 is entered in the table in two places; once for $3 + 5$, and once for $5 + 3$.

+	1	2	3	4	5	6
1			4			
2		4				
3	4				8	
4						
5			8			
6						12

1 Copy the table on to squared paper and complete it.

2 Copy and complete this table. (Use your answer to question 1.)

total scored	2	3	4	5	6	7	8	9	10	11	12
number of ways			3								1

Roll and pay

You will need two fair dice and 24 counters.
Each player starts with 12 counters.
Take it in turns to roll two dice.

Whenever a total of 6 is thrown by **either player**, A gives B a counter.
Whenever a total of 10 is thrown by **either player**, B gives A a counter.
The player who first wins all the counters wins the game.

3 Which player, A or B, is more likely to win, and why?

4 Play the game several times and keep a record of how many times each player wins. Was your answer to question 3 correct?

5 Is the game fair? Give reasons.
Change the rules of the game so that this time, whenever a total of 5 is scored, A gives B a counter, and whenever a total of 9 is scored, B gives A a counter.

6 Which player is more likely to win this game?

7 Test the game again as you did in question 4.

8 Is the second game more fair or less fair than the first game?

1 On the cards

Remove any jokers from a pack of playing cards and examine them.
a How many cards are there in a full pack?
b How many different suits are there?
c What are the names of the suits?
d How many cards are there in each suit?

2 Red and black

Shuffle a full pack of playing cards
Deal out a set of 4 cards.
How many of the 4 are red?
Record this and replace the cards.
Shuffle the pack and try again.
Do this several times and plot a graph
showing how many times you had no reds,
1 red, 2 reds, 3 reds and 4 reds

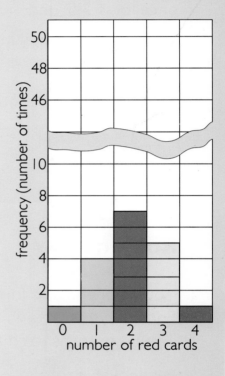

3 Use your graph to answer these questions.
In each set of 4 cards:
a How many reds were most likely?
b How many reds were least likely?
c Are you more likely or less likely to
get 3 reds than 0 reds in each set of 4?

4 Club together

Shuffle a full pack of cards.
Deal out a set of 4 cards.
How many of the 4 are clubs?
Record this and replace the cards.
Shuffle the pack and try again.
Do this several times and plot a graph
showing how many times you had no clubs,
1 club, 2 clubs, 3 clubs and 4 clubs.

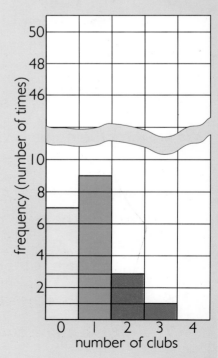

5 Use your graph to put your results in
order of likelihood, starting with the
number of clubs most likely in a set of 4,
down to the number least likely.